· TROPHIES ·

Spelling Practice Book

Grade 5

Harcourt

Orlando   Boston   Dallas   Chicago   San Diego

Visit *The Learning Site!*

www.harcourtschool.com

Theme 5

Theme 6

Making Your Spelling Log

This book gives you a place to keep a word list of your own. It's called a **SPELLING LOG!**

If you need some **IDEAS** for creating your list, just look at what I usually do!

While I read, I look for words that I think are **INTERESTING.** I listen for **NEW WORDS** used by people on radio and television.

I include words that I need to use when I **WRITE,** especially words that are hard for me to spell.

Before I write a word in my Spelling Log, I check the spelling. I look up the word in a **DICTIONARY** or a **THESAURUS,** or I ask for help.

To help me understand and remember the meaning of my word, I write a **DEFINITION,** a **SYNONYM,** or an **ANTONYM.** I also use my word in a sentence.

Harcourt

Making Your Spelling Log

Here's how you use it!

THE SPELLING LOG SECTION of this book is just for you. It's your own list of words that you want to remember. Your Spelling Log has two parts. Here's how to use each part.

Spelling Words to Study

This is where you'll list the Spelling Words you need to study. Include the words you misspelled on the Pretest and any other Spelling Words you aren't sure you can always spell correctly.

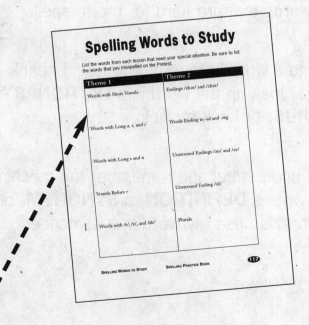

This handy list makes it easy for me to study the words I need to learn!

Harcourt

Making Your Spelling Log

I write a clue beside each word to help me remember it.

My Own Word Collection

You choose the words to list on these pages. Include new words, interesting words, and any other words you want to remember. You decide how to group them, too!

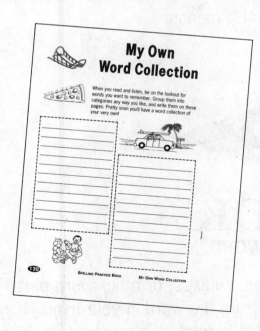

Harcourt

Study Steps to Learn a Word

Check out these steps.

SAY
THE WORD.

Remember when you have heard the word used. Think about what it means.

LOOK
AT THE WORD.

Find any prefixes, suffixes, or other word parts you know. Try to picture the word in your mind. Think of another word that is related in meaning and spelling.

Harcourt

SPELL
THE WORD TO YOURSELF.

Think about the way each sound is spelled. Notice any unusual letter combinations.

WRITE
THE WORD WHILE YOU ARE LOOKING AT IT.

Check the way you have formed your letters. If you have not written the word clearly or correctly, write it again.

CHECK
WHAT YOU HAVE LEARNED.

Cover the word and write it. If you have not spelled the word correctly, practice these steps until you can write it correctly every time.

Harcourt

Words with Short Vowels

▶ **Write the Spelling Word that matches each word or group of words.**

1. a warm piece of clothing _____

2. construct _____

3. restrict _____

4. a female parent _____

5. prepared _____

6. twelve of something _____

7. a place to buy things _____

8. active _____

9. intended _____

10. what milk jugs are made of _____

11. benefit _____

12. a food made of flour _____

13. in front of _____

14. stop _____

15. to keep steady _____

16. learn well _____

▶ **Write the following Spelling Words:** *front, above, does, among.* **Use your best handwriting.**

17. _____ 19. _____

18. _____ 20. _____

Handwriting Tip: Keep the joining stroke high when joining *o* to other letters. Otherwise, an *o* could look like an *a*.

_____

SPELLING PRACTICE BOOK

Harcourt

Name _____

▶ **Read each pair of words. Circle the misspelled word, and then write it correctly.**

1. duzen   dozen   _____

2. ahead   ahed   _____

3. swetter   sweater   _____

4. among   amung   _____

▶ **Proofread the journal entry. Circle the six misspelled words. Then write the words correctly.**

> I worked in a bisy bakery today. I helped everyone get redy to make the bred. The bakery belongs to Chuck's muther, and she doesn't quet working until late in the day. All the time spent dos seem worth it, though.

5. _____   8. _____

6. _____   9. _____

7. _____   10. _____

▶ **Write Spelling Words to complete the sentences.**

I like to watch carpenters (11) _____

new stores. They always look (12) _____

of themselves before climbing a ladder. They

(13) _____ the boards as

they climb. When I stand in

(14) _____ of a store,

I dream about starting a carpentry

(15) _____ one day.

SPELLING WORDS

1. master
2. ahead
3. build
4. front
5. meant
6. bread
7. ready
8. busy
9. quit
10. mother
11. above
12. does
13. advantage
14. business
15. sweater
16. plastic
17. balance
18. limit
19. among
20. dozen

SPELLING STRATEGY

Visualizing

When you want to learn to spell a word, look at it carefully. Then close your eyes and picture the word, concentrating on unusual letter groups.

Harcourt

SPELLING WORDS

1. master
2. ahead
3. build
4. front
5. meant
6. bread
7. ready
8. busy
9. quit
10. mother
11. above
12. does
13. advantage
14. business
15. sweater
16. plastic
17. balance
18. limit
19. among
20. dozen

▶ **Rhyming Riddles** Answer each riddle by writing the Spelling Word that rhymes.

1. What do you call a major accident?

a _____ disaster

2. What is a nickname for Theodore, who is waiting

to go? _____ Teddy

3. What is a "bird of peace" you see in the top of a tree?

a dove _____

4. What do you yell out when you see a mattress in the

road? "Bed _____!"

▶ **Fun with Words** Use Spelling Words to complete the puzzle. Then write the words.

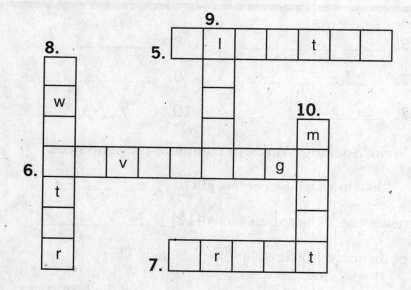

ACROSS

5. _____

6. _____

7. _____

DOWN

8. _____

9. _____

10. _____

Harcourt

Name _____

Words with Long *a*, *e*, and *i*

▶ **Write the Spelling Word that means the opposite of the word or group of words.**

1. unhappy   _____
2. doubts   _____
3. this morning   _____
4. vegetable   _____
5. long   _____
6. departed   _____
7. decreased   _____
8. rarely   _____

▶ **Write the Spelling Word that goes with each definition.**

9. to take in oxygen   _____
10. a tiny amount of computer information   _____
11. happening at the same time   _____
12. fashion   _____
13. made clear   _____
14. in a small way   _____
15. money given for goods or services   _____
16. platter   _____

▶ **Write the following Spelling Words:** *raise, thief, flight, brain*. **Use your best handwriting.**

17. _____
18. _____
19. _____
20. _____

SPELLING WORDS

1. stayed
2. brain
3. thief
4. meat
5. flight
6. style
7. delighted
8. daily
9. breathe
10. meanwhile
11. believes
12. tonight
13. increased
14. explained
15. slightly
16. payment
17. brief
18. tray
19. byte
20. raise

Handwriting Tip: Be careful not to loop the letter *i*. Otherwise, the *i* could look like an *e*.

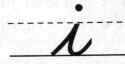

SPELLING WORDS

1. stayed
2. brain
3. thief
4. meat
5. flight
6. style
7. delighted
8. daily
9. breathe
10. meanwhile
11. believes
12. tonight
13. increased
14. explained
15. slightly
16. payment
17. brief
18. tray
19. byte
20. raise

SPELLING STRATEGY
Guessing and Checking

If you're not sure how to spell a word, make a guess. Write the word, and then use a dictionary to see if you're right.

▶ **Proofread the letter. Circle the eight misspelled words. Then write the words correctly.**

Dear Chris,

    Ahoy! I'm on board a freighter tonite, and we're sailing in stile! I wish you could breethe this salty air. You'd like the dayly fishing, too. The captain is delited with the weather and beleaves we'll arrive at our next port early. He says we'll pick up fresh meate and fruit. Menewhile, I'm happy eating fish for breakfast and dinner!

                Amanda

1. _____   5. _____

2. _____   6. _____

3. _____   7. _____

4. _____   8. _____

▶ **Write a Spelling Word to fit in each word group.**

9. grew, expanded, added _____

10. platter, dish, plate _____

11. short, quick, little _____

12. trusts, supposes, thinks _____

13. thrilled, pleased, happy _____

14. remained, lingered, waited _____

Harcourt

Name _____

► **Rhyming Riddles** Answer the riddle by writing a Spelling Word that rhymes.

1. What do you call a robber who steals plant parts?

   a leaf _____

2. What do you call flying beneath the moon and stars?

   night _____

3. What happens when you think too much?

   _____ strain

4. On a partly cloudy day, how does the sun shine?

   _____ brightly

► **Parts of Speech** Many words can be more than one part of speech. Write the Spelling Word that best completes each of these sentences. Then write *n.* if the word is a noun or *v.* if the word is a verb.

5. Will you _____ tomatoes this summer? _____

6. Hurray! Mom got a big _____ in salary! _____

7. What _____ of dress will you wear? _____

8. Look how nicely Jeff can _____ his hair. _____

► **Fun with Words** Inside each word shape, write the Spelling Word that fits.

9.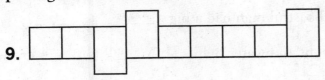

10.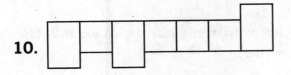

11.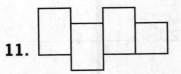

SPELLING WORDS

1. stayed
2. brain
3. thief
4. meat
5. flight
6. style
7. delighted
8. daily
9. breathe
10. meanwhile
11. believes
12. tonight
13. increased
14. explained
15. slightly
16. payment
17. brief
18. tray
19. byte
20. raise

Harcourt

SPELLING WORDS

1. soul
2. smoke
3. move
4. clue
5. fruits
6. lose
7. chose
8. stole
9. prove
10. produce
11. juice
12. drove
13. Tuesday
14. rescue
15. continue
16. issue
17. ego
18. argue
19. cruise
20. toll

Handwriting Tip: Remember to keep the joining stroke high when joining other letters to *o*. Otherwise, the letter *o* could look like an *a*.

_____

Words with Long *o* and *u*

▶ Write the Spelling Word that is the opposite of each word or group of words.

1. be still _____

2. find _____

3. agree _____

4. stop _____

5. deny _____

6. gave _____

7. abandon _____

8. road trip _____

▶ Write the Spelling Word that best completes each sentence.

9. You will need a _____ to answer the riddle.

10. Dairy cows _____ milk.

11. The government will _____ a tax refund.

12. The burning leaves gave off _____.

13. Juanita drank a glass of _____.

14. The boastful man had a big _____.

15. Sunlight and water help _____ to grow.

16. Monday night leads to _____ morning.

▶ Write the following words: *soul, drove, chose, toll.* Use your best handwriting.

17. _____   19. _____

18. _____   20. _____

Harcourt

Name _____

▶ Read the newspaper advertisement. Circle the six misspelled words. Then write the words correctly.

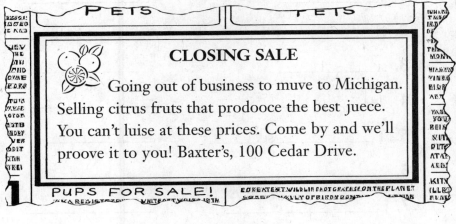

CLOSING SALE

Going out of business to muve to Michigan. Selling citrus fruts that prodooce the best juece. You can't luise at these prices. Come by and we'll proove it to you! Baxter's, 100 Cedar Drive.

PUPS FOR SALE!

1. _____   4. _____

2. _____   5. _____

3. _____   6. _____

▶ Circle the words in each group that look wrong. Write the word that is correct.

7. smoke	smoak	smoce	_____
8. jooce	guice	juice	_____
9. cruze	cruise	croose	_____
10. lose	lozse	lews	_____
11. choase	choes	chose	_____
12. prodduce	produse	produce	_____
13. Tuesday	Tuseday	Toseday	_____
14. continnue	continue	cunntinue	_____

Harcourt

SPELLING WORDS

1. soul
2. smoke
3. move
4. clue
5. fruits
6. lose
7. chose
8. stole
9. prove
10. produce
11. juice
12. drove
13. Tuesday
14. rescue
15. continue
16. issue
17. ego
18. argue
19. cruise
20. toll

SPELLING STRATEGY

Comparing Spellings

If you don't know how to spell a word with a long *o* or a long *u* sound, think about how the sounds are spelled. Choose the spelling that looks right to you.

SPELLING WORDS

1. soul
2. smoke
3. move
4. clue
5. fruits
6. lose
7. chose
8. stole
9. prove
10. produce
11. juice
12. drove
13. Tuesday
14. rescue
15. continue
16. issue
17. ego
18. argue
19. cruise
20. toll

▶ **Missing Vowels** Write the missing vowels to complete the Spelling Words. Then write the words.

1. s_____ _____l   _____

2. cl_____ _____   _____

3. st_____l_____   _____

4. dr_____v_____   _____

5. T_____ _____sd_____y   _____

6. _____ss_____ _____   _____

7. j_____ _____c   _____

8. cr_____ _____s_____   _____

9. fr_____ _____ts   _____

10. pr_____v_____   _____

▶ **Word Scramble** Unscramble each group of letters to write a Spelling Word.

11. ersceu   _____

12. tcouneni _____

13. goe   _____

14. ugrae   _____

15. ltol   _____

16. luce   _____

17. cdopure   _____

Harcourt

Name _____

Vowels Before *r*

▶ **Write a Spelling Word to replace the underlined words.**

I like to **(1)** study **(2)** the past. Sometimes **(3)** certain

events of long ago are like words of **(4)** caution .

(5) Studying the **(6)** sections of our history, I

feel as if I'm **(7)** ready for anything, no matter

how **(8)** rough life may get.

1. _____ 5. _____

2. _____ 6. _____

3. _____ 7. _____

4. _____ 8. _____

▶ **Write a Spelling Word to complete each sentence.**

9. Too much exercise can be _____ .

10. My messy desk is in a state of _____ .

11. A positive _____ always lifts my spirits.

12. When it's cold, I wear my flannel _____ .

13. _____ is the opposite of hope.

14. A _____ eats the acorns in our yard.

15. Every _____ should have a roller coaster.

16. May has a bracelet with silver _____ .

▶ **Write the following words:** *declare, backward, border,*
favored. **Use your best handwriting.**

17. _____ 19. _____

18. _____ 20. _____

SPELLING WORDS

1. parts
2. history
3. warning
4. declare
5. despair
6. shirt
7. learning
8. backward
9. border
10. prepared
11. harsh
12. research
13. carnival
14. particular
15. squirrel
16. harmful
17. charms
18. disorder
19. favored
20. remark

**Handwriting
Tip:** Be sure
that you close
the letter *d* and
do not loop it.
Otherwise, the
d could look
like *cl.*

dad

Harcourt

SPELLING WORDS

1. parts
2. history
3. warning
4. declare
5. despair
6. shirt
7. learning
8. backward
9. border
10. prepared
11. harsh
12. research
13. carnival
14. particular
15. squirrel
16. harmful
17. charms
18. disorder
19. favored
20. remark

SPELLING STRATEGY

Guessing and Checking

When you're not sure how to spell a word, take a guess. After you try your own spelling, check in a dictionary to see whether you are right.

▶ Look at the two spellings. Circle the spelling you think is incorrect. Then check in a dictionary, and write the correctly spelled word.

1. favered   favored   _____

2. particular   partikular   _____

3. remarck   remark   _____

▶ Read the poster for the Science Fair. Circle the five misspelled words. Then write the words correctly.

Science Fair, April 8

Worning! Be prepaired for the lerning experience of your life. You'll discover what's new and what's history. Come to the Fair. Find out how to do resruch yourself!

4. _____   7. _____

5. _____   8. _____

6. _____

▶ Write the Spelling Word that best completes each analogy.

9. *Medicine* is to *helpful* as *poison* is to _____.

10. *Arrangement* is to *order* as *confusion* is to

_____.

11. *Legs* are to *pants* as *arms* are to _____.

12. *River* is to *fish* as *tree* is to _____.

Harcourt

Name_____

SPELLING WORDS

1. parts
2. history
3. warning
4. declare
5. despair
6. shirt
7. learning
8. backward
9. border
10. prepared
11. harsh
12. research
13. carnival
14. particular
15. squirrel
16. harmful
17. charms
18. disorder
19. favored
20. remark

▶ **Numbers and Letters** In each item below, the numbers stand for the letters of a word. Use the code to find and write each letter. You will write a Spelling Word.

1	2	3	4	5	6	7	8	9	10	11	12	13
a	b	c	d	e	f	g	h	i	j	k	l	m

14	15	16	17	18	19	20	21	22	23	24	25	26
n	o	p	q	r	s	t	u	v	w	x	y	z

1. $\overline{16}\ \overline{1}\ \overline{18}\ \overline{20}\ \overline{19}$

2. $\overline{4}\ \overline{5}\ \overline{3}\ \overline{12}\ \overline{1}\ \overline{18}\ \overline{5}$

3. $\overline{2}\ \overline{15}\ \overline{18}\ \overline{4}\ \overline{5}\ \overline{18}$

4. $\overline{8}\ \overline{1}\ \overline{18}\ \overline{19}\ \overline{8}$

5. $\overline{4}\ \overline{5}\ \overline{19}\ \overline{16}\ \overline{1}\ \overline{9}\ \overline{18}$

6. $\overline{8}\ \overline{9}\ \overline{19}\ \overline{20}\ \overline{15}\ \overline{18}\ \overline{25}$

7. $\overline{19}\ \overline{8}\ \overline{9}\ \overline{18}\ \overline{20}$

8. $\overline{16}\ \overline{18}\ \overline{5}\ \overline{16}\ \overline{1}\ \overline{18}\ \overline{5}\ \overline{4}$

9. $\overline{23}\ \overline{1}\ \overline{18}\ \overline{14}\ \overline{9}\ \overline{14}\ \overline{7}$

▶ **Word Scramble** Unscramble each group of letters to write a Spelling Word.

10. lursiqer _____

11. wbadcrak _____

12. scahrm _____

13. varlcina _____

14. strap _____

15. arptulcrai _____

▶ **Rhyming Words** Write the two Spelling Words that rhyme.

16. _____

17. _____

Harcourt

SPELLING WORDS

1. percent
2. absence
3. years
4. refused
5. ancient
6. pressure
7. machine
8. notice
9. scene
10. station
11. social
12. special
13. parachute
14. specialty
15. detention
16. constitution
17. advertisement
18. advise
19. cities
20. chalet

Handwriting Tip: Be sure to slant all letters in the same direction. Keep your paper in the proper position, and hold your pencil or pen correctly.

_____

years

Words with /s/, /z/, and /sh/

▶ **Write the Spelling Word that is the opposite of each given word.**

1. presence _____

2 brand new _____

3. private _____

4. unremarkable _____

5. allowed _____

6. ignore _____

▶ **Write the Spelling Word for each clue.**

7. to counsel _____

8. a portion of something _____

9. periods of 365 days _____

10. towns _____

11. talent _____

12. channel _____

13. engine _____

14. small cottage _____

15. tension _____

16. picture _____

▶ **Write the following words:** *constitution, detention, advertisement, parachute.* **Use your best handwriting.**

17. _____   19. _____

18. _____   20. _____

Harcourt

Name _____

▶ Read each word group, starting with the last word and ending with the first. Then read in the usual direction. Circle the misspelled word. Then write it correctly.

1. is what creates air prechure

   _____

2. the first sene in the play

   _____

3. refuzed to leave the field

   _____

4. trouble with the mashine

   _____

5. an absense from school

   _____

▶ Write a Spelling Word to fit in each word group.

6. friendly, active, lively   _____

7. old, antique, aged   _____

8. towns, villages, communities   _____

9. detect, see, be aware of   _____

10. unique, particular, notable   _____

11. counsel, inform, warn   _____

12. talent, gift, strength   _____

13. days, weeks, months   _____

SPELLING WORDS

1. percent
2. absence
3. years
4. refused
5. ancient
6. pressure
7. machine
8. notice
9. scene
10. station
11. social
12. special
13. parachute
14. specialty
15. detention
16. constitution
17. advertisement
18. advise
19. cities
20. chalet

SPELLING STRATEGY

Reading Backward

When you proofread, start with the last word and end with the first. Then read in the usual direction, slowly, for meaning.

SPELLING WORDS

1. percent
2. absence
3. years
4. refused
5. ancient
6. pressure
7. machine
8. notice
9. scene
10. station
11. social
12. special
13. parachute
14. specialty
15. detention
16. constitution
17. advertisement
18. advise
19. cities
20. chalet

▶ **Fun with Words** Inside each word shape, write the Spelling Word that fits.

1.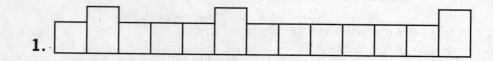

2.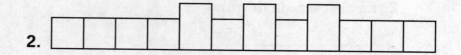

3.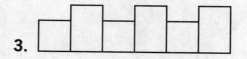

4.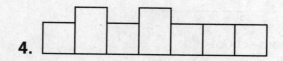

5.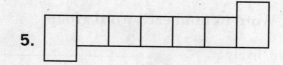

6.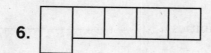

▶ **Missing Vowels** Write the missing vowels to complete the Spelling Words. Then write the words.

7. ____bs____nc____   _____

8. d____t____nt____n   _____

9. p____r____ch____t____   _____

10. p____rc____nt   _____

Harcourt

Practice Test

▶ **Read each sentence. Find the correctly spelled word that completes the sentence. Fill in the oval next to the correct answer.**

1. How is _____ these days?
   - ⬭ business
   - ⬭ busyness
   - ⬭ bisiness

2. The _____ scampered up the tree.
   - ⬭ squirell
   - ⬭ scwirral
   - ⬭ squirrel

3. Have a glass of _____.
   - ⬭ juice
   - ⬭ juce
   - ⬭ jiuce

4. _____ comes before Wednesday.
   - ⬭ Teusday
   - ⬭ Tuesday
   - ⬭ Tuseday

5. You have nothing to _____!
   - ⬭ lose
   - ⬭ loose
   - ⬭ loze

6. Jared did a lot of _____ for his project.
   - ⬭ reserch
   - ⬭ research
   - ⬭ reasearch

7. Don't _____—be hopeful instead!
   - ⬭ despare
   - ⬭ dispair
   - ⬭ despair

8. It takes good _____ to ride a bike.
   - ⬭ ballance
   - ⬭ balance
   - ⬭ balanse

9. "Stop that _____!" cried the man.
   - ⬭ thief
   - ⬭ theaf
   - ⬭ theif

10. Please buy a _____ fresh eggs at the market.
    - ⬭ dozan
    - ⬭ duzzen
    - ⬭ dozen

11. I _____ to rake the leaves.
    - ⬭ ment
    - ⬭ meant
    - ⬭ meandt

12. How _____ the machine work?
    - ⬭ dos
    - ⬭ dus
    - ⬭ does

Name _____

▶ **Read each sentence. If the underlined word is misspelled, fill in the oval next to the correct spelling. If the word is spelled correctly, fill in the third oval.**

1. One way to relax is to <u>breithe</u> deeply.
   - ⬭ breathe   ⬭ brethe   ⬭ correct

2. "This won't take long," the nurse <u>explained</u>.
   - ⬭ explaned   ⬭ explened   ⬭ correct

3. Do you prefer a <u>particulor</u> flavor?
   - ⬭ particuler   ⬭ particular   ⬭ correct

4. Who will <u>rescue</u> the cat from the roof?
   - ⬭ reskue   ⬭ rescu   ⬭ correct

5. <u>Meanwile</u>, we will wait in the hall.
   - ⬭ Meanwhile   ⬭ Mean while   ⬭ correct

6. Did you see the <u>advertisment</u> for the new movie?
   - ⬭ advertizement   ⬭ advertisement   ⬭ correct

7. The skydiver's <u>parashute</u> is brightly colored.
   - ⬭ parachute   ⬭ perachute   ⬭ correct

8. Did anyone <u>notice</u> Charlotte's new glasses?
   - ⬭ nottice   ⬭ notise   ⬭ correct

9. Take <u>advantage</u> of the opportunity.
   - ⬭ advandage   ⬭ advandege   ⬭ correct

10. The <u>anshient</u> vase is very valuable.
    - ⬭ ankshent   ⬭ ancient   ⬭ correct

11. I wear a green <u>shirt</u> with my uniform.
    - ⬭ shert   ⬭ shiert   ⬭ correct

12. That car is five <u>yeers</u> old.
    - ⬭ years   ⬭ yeares   ⬭ correct

Name _____

Endings /zhər/ and /chər/

▶ **Write the Spelling Word that goes with each mini-definition.**

1. a combination of two or more substances _____

2. something that was built _____

3. to find or check the size _____

4. to catch an animal _____

5. all the beliefs and customs of a group of people _____

6. a field where animals live _____

7. poems, novels, and plays _____

8. chest full of jewels _____

9. young; not yet developed _____

10. early; before its time _____

11. the degree of heat _____

12. a photograph _____

13. a governing body _____

14. chairs, tables, and beds _____

15. a person's written name _____

16. a feeling of enjoyment _____

▶ **Write the following Spelling Words:** *feature, creature, adventure, leisure.* **Use your best handwriting.**

17. _____   19. _____

18. _____   20. _____

SPELLING WORDS

1. treasure
2. capture
3. feature
4. pleasure
5. measure
6. creature
7. picture
8. adventure
9. mixture
10. structure
11. pasture
12. culture
13. literature
14. furniture
15. temperature
16. legislature
17. immature
18. leisure
19. premature
20. signature

Handwriting Tip: Tall letters should touch both the top and the bottom line. Short letters should touch the imaginary midline and the bottom line.

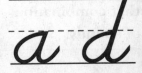

Harcourt

SPELLING WORDS

1. treasure
2. capture
3. feature
4. pleasure
5. measure
6. creature
7. picture
8. adventure
9. mixture
10. structure
11. pasture
12. culture
13. literature
14. furniture
15. temperature
16. legislature
17. immature
18. leisure
19. premature
20. signature

SPELLING STRATEGY

Ending Syllables

When you're not sure how to spell the last syllable of a word, pronounce the word carefully. Write the letters that usually make that combination of sounds.

▶ **Read each set of spellings. Circle the misspellings, and then write the correct spelling on the line.**

1. structsure   structure   strucsure   _____

2. capture   capsure   captsure   _____

3. picsure   picture   pichure   _____

4. culsure   cultchure   culture   _____

5. measure   meazure   meature   _____

6. pleazure   pleature   pleasure   _____

7. leesure   leisure   leshure   _____

8. ferniture   furnachure   furniture   _____

▶ **Read the letter. Circle the seven misspelled words. Then write the words correctly.**

Dear Mike,

What an advensure this camping trip is. We slept in a pastsure last night and heard a creachure prowling right near us. I kept trying to pikture what it looked like, but each featsure I imagined scared me too much. I'll have a treazure chest full of things to share with you when I get home. The trip has been a mixtsure of fun and hard work. Next year, how would you like to come with us?

Sam

9. _____   13. _____

10. _____   14. _____

11. _____   15. _____

12. _____

Harcourt

Name _____

▶ **Fun with Words** Use Spelling Words to complete the word chain. Then write the words.

SPELLING WORDS

1. treasure
2. capture
3. feature
4. pleasure
5. measure
6. creature
7. picture
8. adventure
9. mixture
10. structure
11. pasture
12. culture
13. literature
14. furniture
15. temperature
16. legislature
17. immature
18. leisure
19. premature
20. signature

ACROSS	DOWN
2. _____	1. _____
5. _____	3. _____
6. _____	4. _____

(crossword grid with letters: 1. p, 3. f, 4., 5., 2., t, 6., s)

▶ **Mystery Vowels** For each ?, think of the missing vowel. Then write the Spelling Word.

7. l?t?r?t?r? _____

8. s?gn?t?r? _____

9. t?mp?r?t?r? _____

10. ?mm?t?r? _____

11. pr?m?t?r? _____

12. l?g?sl?t?r? _____

Harcourt

Words Ending in *-ed* and *-ing*

▶ Add *-ed* or *-ing* to each word to make a Spelling Word.

1. practice _____

2. charge _____

3. move _____

4. injure _____

5. try _____

6. die _____

7. carry _____

8. spy _____

9. taste _____

10. receive _____

▶ Write the Spelling Word that goes with each mini-definition.

11. counted up _____

12. cooked in hot oil _____

13. picked up and moved _____

14. imagined and made _____

15. gave supplies to _____

16. understood; knew _____

▶ Write the following Spelling Words: *lying, revising, becoming, wearing*. Use your best handwriting.

17. _____ 19. _____

18. _____ 20. _____

Handwriting Tip: Be sure to make your letters and joining strokes smooth and even.

spied

Harcourt

Name_____

▶ **Read each pair of words. Circle the word that is misspelled, and write the correct spelling on the line.**

1. wearing   waring   _____

2. revising   revizing   _____

3. providded   provided   _____

4. realized   realised   _____

5. tallyed   tallied   _____

6. spied   spyed   _____

▶ **Write the Spelling Word that best completes each analogy.**

7. *Giving* is to *taking* as *living* is to _____.

8. *Shining* is to *glowing* as *attempting* is to

    _____.

9. *Imagining* is to *thinking* as *walking* is to

    _____.

10. *Helping* is to *aiding* as *changing* is to _____.

11. *Stay* is to *leave* as *took away* is to _____.

▶ **Write the Spelling Words in alphabetical order.**

charged	practicing	lying
realized	created	

12. _____   15. _____

13. _____   16. _____

14. _____

Harcourt

SPELLING WORDS

1. charged
2. spied
3. moving
4. trying
5. practicing
6. injured
7. carrying
8. tasted
9. receiving
10. becoming
11. lying
12. dying
13. realized
14. provided
15. fried
16. created
17. tallied
18. carried
19. revising
20. wearing

SPELLING STRATEGY

Working Together

When you proofread, work with a partner. Read the words aloud as your partner looks at the spellings. Then trade jobs.

SPELLING WORDS

1. charged
2. spied
3. moving
4. trying
5. practicing
6. injured
7. carrying
8. tasted
9. receiving
10. becoming
11. lying
12. dying
13. realized
14. provided
15. fried
16. created
17. tallied
18. carried
19. revising
20. wearing

▶ **Word Search** Find eight Spelling Words hidden in the puzzle. Circle each word, and then write it.

```
j k m n d y i n g y u c o
v b b b k l o u h g b a s
u r e d g v r e g f c r i
r e c e i v i n g t a r n
v b o t y u i o p m w y j
e d m v b h y u c o p i u
c t i c z n g z x v v n r
d t n u i o p l y i n g e
a q g e r t y l l n i o d
p r a c t i c i n g f p l
```

1. _____ 5. _____

2. _____ 6. _____

3. _____ 7. _____

4. _____ 8. _____

▶ **Word Operations** Write the Spelling Words that you find when you perform the math operations.

9. practice − e + ing = _____

10. try + ing = _____

11. injure − e + ed = _____

12. spy − y + i + ed = _____

▶ **Word Scramble** Unscramble each set of letters to write a Spelling Word.

13. asttde _____

14. drefi _____

15. racidre _____

Harcourt

Name _____

Unstressed Endings /ən/ and /ər/

▶ Write the Spelling Word that matches each word or group of words.

1. great-great-grandmother _____

2. a farming machine _____

3. closes a shirt _____

4. a part of a book _____

5. a place to watch a movie _____

6. older _____

7. can't be seen _____

8. born in the United States _____

▶ Write a Spelling Word to complete each analogy.

9. *Airport* is to *planes* as _____ is to *ships*.

10. *Mother* is to *daughter* as _____ is to *son*.

11. *Shape* is to *square* as _____ is to *red*.

12. *Seen* is to *see* as _____ is to *take*.

13. *Old* is to *new* as _____ is to *thawed*.

14. *Silver* is to *shiny gray* as _____ is to *shiny yellow*.

15. *Pie* is to *dessert* as _____ is to *dinner*.

16. *Hot* is to *temperature* as *rainy* is to _____.

▶ Write the following Spelling Words: *beckon, comparison, turban, cannon.* Use your best handwriting.

17. _____   19. _____

18. _____   20. _____

SPELLING WORDS

1. American
2. frozen
3. button
4. chapter
5. tractor
6. golden
7. taken
8. harbor
9. father
10. color
11. ancestor
12. hidden
13. hamburger
14. theater
15. weather
16. beckon
17. cannon
18. comparison
19. elder
20. turban

Handwriting Tip: Be sure to use just one overcurve joining stroke before forming the letter *n*. Otherwise, the *n* could look like an *m*.

Harcourt

SPELLING WORDS

1. American
2. frozen
3. button
4. chapter
5. tractor
6. golden
7. taken
8. harbor
9. father
10. color
11. ancestor
12. hidden
13. hamburger
14. theater
15. weather
16. beckon
17. cannon
18. comparison
19. elder
20. turban

SPELLING STRATEGY

Writing Aloud

When you are learning to spell a word, it is sometimes helpful to say each letter aloud as you practice writing the word.

▶ Circle each misspelled word. Then, as you write the word correctly on the line, say each letter aloud.

1. elder   eldar   _____
2. ansector   ancestor   _____
3. comparrison comparison   _____
4. cannon   cannan   _____
5. turbin   turban   _____
6. tractor   tracter   _____

▶ Proofread the directions. Circle the six misspelled words. Then write the words correctly.

DIRECTIONS TO AMY'S HOUSE

Travel east on Sixth Street until you see a big goldon sign that is the shape and coler of a lion. Turn right on Columbus Street toward the harber. The street name is hiddin by trees, so watch for it. When you get to 281 Columbus, you'll see an Americon flag. Press the doorbell butten, and I'll come running!

7. _____   10. _____
8. _____   11. _____
9. _____   12. _____

▶ Write the Spelling Word that is the opposite of each given word.

13. thawed _____   15. given _____
14. mother _____   16. revealed _____

Harcourt

Name _____

► **Missing Vowels** Write the missing vowels to complete the Spelling Words. Then write the words.

1. ch____pt____r   _____

2. f____th____r   _____

3. h____dd____n   _____

4. tr____ct____r   _____

5. h____mb____rg____r   _____

6. w____ ____th____r   _____

► **Sentence Sense** Write the Spelling Word that best completes the sentence.

7. If you mix blue and yellow, what _____ do you get?

8. A _____ is missing from my jacket.

9. I have _____ my books to the library.

10. The lights in the _____ dimmed as the curtain rose.

11. I hope this pleasant _____ continues throughout our vacation.

12. Did Mother _____ us to come in for dinner?

► **Base Words** Write the Spelling Word that is a form of the word given.

13. freeze   _____

14. hide   _____

15. take   _____

SPELLING WORDS

1. American
2. frozen
3. button
4. chapter
5. tractor
6. golden
7. taken
8. harbor
9. father
10. color
11. ancestor
12. hidden
13. hamburger
14. theater
15. weather
16. beckon
17. cannon
18. comparison
19. elder
20. turban

Harcourt

SPELLING WORDS

1. level
2. double
3. metal
4. evil
5. travel
6. couple
7. needle
8. battle
9. candle
10. article
11. equal
12. civil
13. capital
14. original
15. individual
16. material
17. angel
18. camel
19. illegal
20. stencil

Unstressed Ending /əl/

▶ **Write the Spelling Word that best completes each of these sentences.**

1. Would you like to _____ by dogsled?

2. Sleds often have _____ runners.

3. The dogs prefer _____ ground.

4. Every _____ on the sled adds to the total weight.

5. The journey takes a _____ of days.

6. Each _____ team sets its own pace.

7. Waterproof _____ will keep you dry.

▶ **Write the Spelling Word that matches each word or group of words.**

8. twice as much _____

9. fight _____

10. the same _____

11. sharp sewing tool _____

12. polite _____

13. wicked _____

14. source of light _____

15. against the law _____

16. first of its kind _____

▶ **Write the following Spelling Words:** *angel, camel, stencil, capital.* **Use your best handwriting.**

17. _____   19. _____

18. _____   20. _____

Handwriting Tip: Be sure that tall letters, such as *l*, touch the top line. Otherwise, an *l* might look like an *e*.

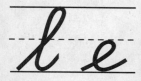

Harcourt

Name_____

▶ **The missing syllable of each Spelling Word below is pronounced /əl/. Think of the missing letters. Then write the Spelling Word.**

1. civ____ rights   _____

2. newspaper artic____   _____

3. a met____ spoon   _____

4. draw using a stenc____   _____

5. cross the desert on a cam____   _____

6. enough materi____ for a·blanket _____

▶ **Read the paragraph that Charlie wrote about patriots. Circle the six misspelled words. Then write the words correctly.**

The patriots wanted to stop the eval of taxation and fought for equil representation. They were willing to battel for their freedom. By the light of a candil, Thomas Jefferson struggled to write a declaration that the colonies were now independent states. Many patriots had to travle long distances to be present at each session of the Continental Congress. Their levle of courage is still admired today.

7. _____   10. _____

8. _____   11. _____

9. _____   12. _____

SPELLING WORDS

1. level
2. double
3. metal
4. evil
5. travel
6. couple
7. needle
8. battle
9. candle
10. article
11. equal
12. civil
13. capital
14. original
15. individual
16. material
17. angel
18. camel
19. illegal
20. stencil

SPELLING STRATEGY

Syllable Patterns

When you are learning to spell a two-syllable word, study the pattern of letters in the final syllable. Look for a similar pattern in other words.

Harcourt

SPELLING WORDS

1. level
2. double
3. metal
4. evil
5. travel
6. couple
7. needle
8. battle
9. candle
10. article
11. equal
12. civil
13. capital
14. original
15. individual
16. material
17. angel
18. camel
19. illegal
20. stencil

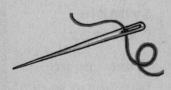

▶ **Break the Code** In each item below, the numbers stand for the letters of a word. Use the code to find and write each letter. You will write a Spelling Word.

1	2	3	4	5	6	7	8	9	10	11	12	13
a	b	c	d	e	f	g	h	i	j	k	l	m

14	15	16	17	18	19	20	21	22	23	24	25	26
n	o	p	q	r	s	t	u	v	w	x	y	z

1. ____ ____ ____ ____ ____ ____
   4 15 21 2 12 5

4. ____ ____ ____ ____ ____
   3 9 22 9 12

2. ____ ____ ____ ____ ____ ____ ____
   1 18 20 9 3 12 5

5. ____ ____ ____ ____ ____
   1 14 7 5 12

3. ____ ____ ____ ____ ____ ____
   3 15 21 16 12 5

6. ____ ____ ____ ____ ____ ____ ____ ____
   15 18 9 7 9 14 1 12

▶ **Word Scramble** Unscramble each group of letters to write a Spelling Word.

7. edenle _____

8. leamt _____

9. lcpiata _____

10. uidnalidvi _____

▶ **Analogies** Write the Spelling Word that best completes the analogy.

11. *Ink* is to *pen* as *thread* is to _____.

12. *Book* is to *chapter* as *war* is to _____.

13. *Wet* is to *dry* as *good* is to _____.

14. *Three* is to *triple* as *two* is to _____.

15. *Permitted* is to *forbidden* as *lawful* is to

_____.

Harcourt

Name _____

Plurals

▶ Write the Spelling Word that is the plural form of the singular noun.

1. wave _____
2. roof _____
3. crisis _____
4. hero _____
5. knife _____

6. datum _____
7. army _____
8. medium _____
9. tomato _____
10. loaf _____

▶ Write the Spelling Word that goes with each mini-definition.

11. movies you can watch at home _____

12. animals that can pull a wagon _____

13. important, up-to-date communications _____

14. what you make when blowing out birthday candles _____

15. fruits that grow on bushes _____

16. breathes, eats, grows _____

▶ Write the following Spelling Words: *bacteria, messages, canoes, pianos*. Use your best handwriting.

17. _____
18. _____
19. _____
20. _____

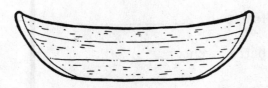

SPELLING WORDS

1. crises
2. knives
3. media
4. roofs
5. pianos
6. waves
7. wishes
8. armies
9. briefs
10. videos
11. heroes
12. data
13. bacteria
14. oxen
15. tomatoes
16. canoes
17. berries
18. loaves
19. lives
20. messages

Handwriting Tip: Keep the joining stroke on the letter *a* low, so that it does not look like an *o*.

Harcourt

SPELLING WORDS

1. crises
2. knives
3. media
4. roofs
5. pianos
6. waves
7. wishes
8. armies
9. briefs
10. videos
11. heroes
12. data
13. bacteria
14. oxen
15. tomatoes
16. canoes
17. berries
18. loaves
19. lives
20. messages

SPELLING STRATEGY

Using a Dictionary

After spelling a word, look at it carefully. If you are not sure that it is spelled correctly, check in a dictionary.

▶ Read each pair of words. Circle the one that is misspelled, and write the correct spelling on the line. If you are not sure which is correct, check it in a dictionary.

1. tomatos   tomatoes   _____

2. briefs   breifs   _____

3. berries   berrys   _____

4. messeges   messages   _____

5. bacteria   bakteria   _____

▶ Read the sign below. Circle each singular word that should be plural. Then write its plural form.

```
╔══════════════════════════════════════╗
         GOING-OUT-OF-BUSINESS SALE
   Many trade crisis are forcing us out of business.
 There will be army of people here Saturday, so come
 early! Don't call us hero for selling everything at low
 prices. We need the sales! We'll be offering piano, video,
 and more. Best wish to you, our customers!
╚══════════════════════════════════════╝
```

6. _____   9. _____

7. _____   10. _____

8. _____   11. _____

▶ Write Spelling Words to complete the items below.

12. one ox, eight _____

13. one canoe, three _____

14. one loaf, two _____

15. one berry, twenty _____

16. one roof, two _____

17. one tomato, ten _____

Harcourt

Name _____

▶ **Rhyming Riddles** Answer the riddle by writing the
Spelling Word that rhymes.

1. What are the caverns that rough water crashes into?

caves of _____

2. What are biographies of cutting tools?

lives of _____

3. What are mistakes made on housetops?

goofs on _____

4. What are the hopes of plates? _____ of dishes

5. What are important reports given to the President?

the Chief's _____

▶ **Mystery Vowels** For each ?, think of the missing
vowel. Then write the Spelling Word.

6. d?t? _____

7. m?d?? _____

8. h?r??s _____

9. cr?s?s _____

10. t?m?t??s _____

11. m?ss?g?s _____

12. b?ct?r?? _____

▶ **Word Scramble** Unscramble each group of letters to
write a Spelling Word.

13. isanpo _____

14. sodevi _____

15. smaseseg _____

16. neiksv _____

17. seaonc _____

18. velis _____

SPELLING WORDS

1. crises
2. knives
3. media
4. roofs
5. pianos
6. waves
7. wishes
8. armies
9. briefs
10. videos
11. heroes
12. data
13. bacteria
14. oxen
15. tomatoes
16. canoes
17. berries
18. loaves
19. lives
20. messages

Harcourt

Name _____

Practice Test

▶ **Read each sentence. Find the correctly spelled word that completes the sentence. Fill in the oval next to the correct answer.**

1. Let's plant _____ in the garden.
   ⬭ tomatoos   ⬭ tomatoes   ⬭ tomatos

2. Stealing is _____.
   ⬭ ellegle   ⬭ illigal   ⬭ illegal

3. We _____ up late last night.
   ⬭ stayed   ⬭ staed   ⬭ stade

4. He _____ you are telling the truth.
   ⬭ beleives   ⬭ beleves   ⬭ believes

5. The judge _____ the score.
   ⬭ tallyed   ⬭ tallied   ⬭ talleed

6. There is _____ coming out of the fireplace.
   ⬭ smoke   ⬭ smok   ⬭ smoak

7. That nature hike was quite an _____!
   ⬭ advenchure   ⬭ advinture   ⬭ adventure

8. We _____ know each other.
   ⬭ bairly   ⬭ barely   ⬭ bearly

9. I like that _____ from the movie.
   ⬭ scene   ⬭ sene   ⬭ sceen

10. After band practice, it is nice to have _____.
    ⬭ silence   ⬭ silens   ⬭ scilence

11. The _____ of bread just came out of the oven.
    ⬭ laoves   ⬭ loaves   ⬭ loafs

12. I'm going to order a _____ for lunch.
    ⬭ hamberger   ⬭ hamburgre   ⬭ hamburger

42 SPELLING PRACTICE BOOK   REVIEW

Name _____

▶ **Read each sentence. Decide which underlined word is misspelled. Fill in the oval below that word.**

1. We <u>realized</u> the boats were <u>moveing</u> across the <u>harbor</u>.
   ◯   ◯   ◯

2. Did the <u>picksure</u> <u>capture</u> your best <u>feature</u>?
   ◯   ◯   ◯

3. <u>Father</u> set out <u>mettel</u> <u>knives</u> and forks.
   ◯   ◯   ◯

4. He <u>injured</u> his back <u>carrying</u> the heavy <u>materiel</u>.
   ◯   ◯   ◯

5. <u>American</u> <u>heroes</u> have fought in <u>armies</u>.
   ◯   ◯   ◯

6. What <u>coler</u> is the <u>creature</u> in <u>chapter</u> one?
   ◯   ◯   ◯

7. The <u>couple</u> wrote an <u>artical</u> about <u>culture</u>.
   ◯   ◯   ◯

8. The <u>tractor</u> was <u>hiden</u> inside a rickety <u>structure</u>.
   ◯   ◯   ◯

9. Add an <u>equel</u> <u>measure</u> to double the <u>mixture</u>.
   ◯   ◯   ◯

10. My <u>ancestor</u> used to <u>travle</u> the ocean <u>waves</u>.
    ◯   ◯   ◯

11. Write your <u>signachure</u> on each of these <u>briefs</u> and <u>messages</u>.
    ◯   ◯   ◯

12. Keep the <u>berries</u> at a <u>frozin</u> <u>temperature</u>.
    ◯   ◯   ◯

13. The author in the <u>turbun</u> <u>created</u> an <u>original</u> work of art.
    ◯   ◯   ◯

14. Which <u>individual</u> <u>provided</u> the <u>furnature</u> for the house?
    ◯   ◯   ◯

SPELLING WORDS

1. island
2. design
3. calm
4. column
5. sword
6. half
7. yolk
8. walked
9. talk
10. chalk
11. wrinkled
12. wrong
13. autumn
14. solemn
15. aisle
16. foreign
17. lightning
18. benign
19. glistened
20. resign

Handwriting Tip: Be sure to close the letter *a* at the top, or the *a* could look like a *u*.

_____

Words with "Silent" Letters

▶ **Write the Spelling Word that goes with each mini-definition.**

1. a drawing or sketch _____

2. a post that supports a roof _____

3. not correct _____

4. the yellow part of an egg _____

5. one of two equal parts _____

6. a weapon with a blade _____

7. land surrounded by water _____

8. harmless and mild _____

9. another name for fall _____

10. from another country _____

11. serious and grave _____

12. quiet and peaceful _____

▶ **Choose a Spelling Word to complete each sentence.**

13. Please iron these _____ shirts.

14. Did the mayor _____ from office?

15. The snow _____ in the moonlight.

16. Did you see that bolt of _____ ?

▶ **Write the following Spelling Words:** *walked, talk, aisle, chalk.* **Use your best handwriting.**

17. _____ 19. _____

18. _____ 20. _____

Harcourt

Name_____

▶ Read the message found floating at sea. Circle the six misspelled words. Then write the words correctly.

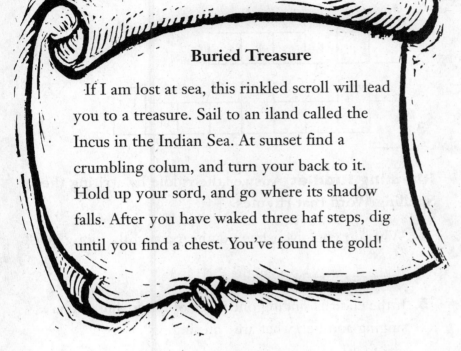

Buried Treasure

If I am lost at sea, this rinkled scroll will lead you to a treasure. Sail to an iland called the Incus in the Indian Sea. At sunset find a crumbling colum, and turn your back to it. Hold up your sord, and go where its shadow falls. After you have waked three haf steps, dig until you find a chest. You've found the gold!

1. _____   4. _____

2. _____   5. _____

3. _____   6. _____

▶ Put a caret (^) in each word below to show where a "silent" letter has been omitted. Then write the word correctly.

7. y o k

_____

8. s o l e m

_____

9. b e n i n

_____

10. d e s i n

_____

11. r e s i n

_____

12. f o r e i n

_____

Harcourt

SPELLING WORDS

1. island
2. design
3. calm
4. column
5. sword
6. half
7. yolk
8. walked
9. talk
10. chalk
11. wrinkled
12. wrong
13. autumn
14. solemn
15. aisle
16. foreign
17. lightning
18. benign
19. glistened
20. resign

SPELLING STRATEGY

Missing Letters

It's easy to forget "silent" letters when writing words like the Spelling Words. Proofread carefully to make sure that you've included them.

SPELLING WORDS

1. island
2. design
3. calm
4. column
5. sword
6. half
7. yolk
8. walked
9. talk
10. chalk
11. wrinkled
12. wrong
13. autumn
14. solemn
15. aisle
16. foreign
17. lightning
18. benign
19. glistened
20. resign

▶ **Fun with Words** Inside each word shape, write the Spelling Word that fits.

1.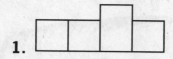

2.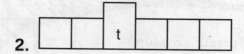

3.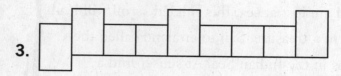

▶ **Rhyming Riddles** Answer the riddle by writing the Spelling Word that rhymes.

4. What do you give when you hear a slightly funny joke?

   _____ a laugh

5. If the choir is singing one piece of music, but you are singing another, what are you singing?

   the _____ song

6. What do you have when many storage cabinets are lined up in a hallway? a file _____

▶ **Word Scramble** Unscramble each group of letters to write a Spelling Word.

7. ilwekdrn   _____

8. ahkcl   _____

9. gtlnihngi   _____

10. alkt   _____

11. nriseg   _____

12. msonel   _____

Harcourt

Name_____

Compound Words

SPELLING WORDS

1. basketball
2. seventy-five
3. rock band
4. everybody
5. fireplace
6. anything
7. takeoff
8. skateboard
9. homework
10. two-thirds
11. high school
12. railroad
13. motorcycle
14. vice president
15. strawberry
16. freeway
17. car pool
18. comic strip
19. fine arts
20. forty-two

▶ **Write the Spelling Word that matches each clue.**

1. when a jet leaves the airport _____

2. two out of three _____

3. where you go after middle school _____

4. it saves fuel and highway space _____

5. second in command _____

6. a source of warmth _____

7. forty plus two _____

8. a bike with an engine _____

9. ride it while wearing a helmet and pads _____

10. teachers assign it _____

11. a thing of any kind _____

12. funny part of the newspaper _____

13. group of musicians _____

14. all people in a group _____

15. a busy road _____

16. another word for train _____

▶ **Write the following Spelling Words:** *basketball, fine arts, seventy-five, strawberry.* **Use your best handwriting.**

17. _____   19. _____

18. _____   20. _____

Handwriting Tip: Remember that tall letters should touch the top line and the bottom line. Most short letters should touch an imaginary midline and the bottom line.

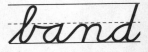

Harcourt

SPELLING WORDS

1. basketball
2. seventy-five
3. rock band
4. everybody
5. fireplace
6. anything
7. takeoff
8. skateboard
9. homework
10. two-thirds
11. high school
12. railroad
13. motorcycle
14. vice president
15. strawberry
16. freeway
17. car pool
18. comic strip
19. fine arts
20. forty-two

SPELLING STRATEGY

Compound Words

A compound word has two or more words. Most compound words are written as one word. Some have a hyphen or a space between the words.

► **Read the journal entry. Circle the ten misspelled words. Then write the words correctly.**

Evrybody pitched in to make our school festival a big success. More than seventyfive people volunteered. "Is there annything I can do to help?" was heard all morning long.

After a picnic lunch, students from the highschool demonstrated skaitboard safety and skills. They explained that twothirds of all injuries could be prevented by the use of safety equipment.

Then some parents, teachers, and students formed basket-ball teams. Other people danced to the rockband that performed at one end of the field. Others looked up to watch the jets climb after takoff from the nearby airport.

At the end of the day, volunteers helped clean up. Then my parents and I went home, and Mom built a fire in the fire-place. I sat there for a long time, just watching the flames.

1. _____   6. _____

2. _____   7. _____

3. _____   8. _____

4. _____   9. _____

5. _____   10. _____

►**Unscramble each group of letters to write a Spelling Word.**

11. reyawfe _____

12. ocaporl _____

13. ecymlotroc _____

14. aetrbryswr _____

Harcourt

Name _____

▶ **Double Trouble** Form a Spelling Word by writing a second word next to each word. Then write the compound word.

1. high _____   _____

2. _____ five   _____

3. _____ thing   _____

4. _____ place   _____

5. rock _____   _____

6. rail _____   _____

7. _____ president _____

8. _____ arts   _____

9. comic _____   _____

10. _____ two   _____

▶ **Fun with Words** Inside each word shape, write the Spelling Word that fits.

11.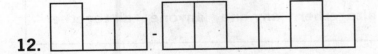

12.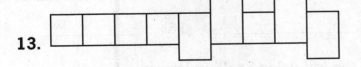

13.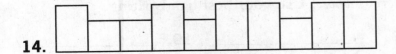

14.

SPELLING WORDS

1. basketball
2. seventy-five
3. rock band
4. everybody
5. fireplace
6. anything
7. takeoff
8. skateboard
9. homework
10. two-thirds
11. high school
12. railroad
13. motorcycle
14. vice president
15. strawberry
16. freeway
17. car pool
18. comic strip
19. fine arts
20. forty-two

Harcourt

Name_____

1. anyway
2. any way
3. all right
4. every one
5. everyone
6. already
7. all ready
8. a lot
9. its
10. it's
11. your
12. you're
13. who's
14. whose
15. there's
16. theirs
17. anyone
18. any one
19. altogether
20. all together

Troublesome Words and Phrases

▶ **Write two Spelling Words to complete each sentence.**

Since I'm here **(1)** _____, I'll be happy

to help in **(2)** _____ I can.

Now that **(3)** _____ here, we'll be happy

to have **(4)** _____ help.

The set decorations took **(5)** _____ of work,

but they look **(6)** _____ now.

Before **(7)** _____ time to raise the curtain,
this backdrop has to be able to stand up on

(8) _____ own.

Two actors are **(9)** _____ on the stage, and

the others are **(10)** _____ for their cues.

(11) _____ gave us a standing ovation after

(12) _____ of the acts.

▶ **Write the Spelling Words in alphabetical order.**

altogether	any one	anyone	all together

13. _____ 15. _____

14. _____ 16. _____

▶ **Write the following Spelling Words:** *who's, theirs, there's, whose.* **Use your best handwriting.**

17. _____ 19. _____

18. _____ 20. _____

Handwriting Tip: Be sure to slant all your letters in the same direction, keep your paper in the proper position, and hold your pencil or pen correctly.

a lot

Name _____

▶ **Think about the meaning of each sentence. Underline the correct Spelling Word in parentheses. Then write it on the line.**

1. This book has lost (**its, it's**) jacket. _____

2. Everything was (**all ready, already**) for the party.

   _____

3. (**Who's, Whose**) going to feed the fish?

   _____

4. (**There's, Theirs**) only one day left until spring break.

   _____

5. Working (**all together, altogether**), we collected

   1,367 cans for the food drive. _____

▶ **Proofread Anne's letter to Meg. Circle the six misspelled words or phrases. Then write the words correctly.**

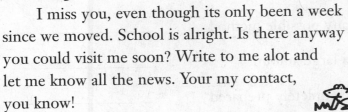

Dear Meg,
     I miss you, even though its only been a week since we moved. School is alright. Is there anyway you could visit me soon? Write to me alot and let me know all the news. Your my contact, you know!

                    You're friend,
                    Anne

6. _____   9. _____

7. _____   10. _____

8. _____   11. _____

SPELLING WORDS

1. anyway
2. any way
3. all right
4. every one
5. everyone
6. already
7. all ready
8. a lot
9. its
10. it's
11. your
12. you're
13. who's
14. whose
15. there's
16. theirs
17. anyone
18. any one
19. altogether
20. all together

SPELLING STRATEGY

Word Meaning

Some words that sound the same are spelled in different ways depending on their meaning. Remember to think about the meanings of the words and the sentence as you write.

SPELLING WORDS

1. anyway
2. any way
3. all right
4. every one
5. everyone
6. already
7. all ready
8. a lot
9. its
10. it's
11. your
12. you're
13. who's
14. whose
15. there's
16. theirs
17. anyone
18. any one
19. altogether
20. all together

▶ **Break the Code** In each item below, the numbers stand for the letters of a word. Use the code to find and write each letter. You will write Spelling Words.

1	2	3	4	5	6	7	8	9	10	11	12	13
a	b	c	d	e	f	g	h	i	j	k	l	m

14	15	16	17	18	19	20	21	22	23	24	25	26
n	o	p	q	r	s	t	u	v	w	x	y	z

1. $\overline{1}$ $\overline{14}$ $\overline{25}$ $\overline{23}$ $\overline{1}$ $\overline{25}$

2. $\overline{1}$ $\overline{12}$ $\overline{18}$ $\overline{5}$ $\overline{1}$ $\overline{4}$ $\overline{25}$

3. $\overline{25}$ $\overline{15}$ $\overline{21}$ $\overline{18}$

4. $\overline{9}$ $\overline{20}$ $\overline{19}$

5. $\overline{1}$ $\overline{14}$ $\overline{25}$ $\overline{15}$ $\overline{14}$ $\overline{5}$

▶ **Dictionary** Write the Spelling Word that goes with each mini-definition.

6. all the items in a group _____

7. any possible method _____

8. a large amount _____

9. completely prepared _____

10. belonging to them _____

▶ **Fill in the Blank** Write the Spelling Word that best completes the sentence.

11 _____ person can do it alone.

12. _____ book is this?

13. _____, the present cost twenty dollars.

SPELLING PRACTICE BOOK

LESSON 13

Harcourt

Name _____

Words with *-ant* and *-ent*

▶ **Write the Spelling Word that is the opposite of each given word.**

1. past _____

2. obnoxious _____

3. educated _____

4. near _____

5. guilty _____

6. present _____

7. uninformed _____

8. restless _____

9. outdated _____

10. delayed _____

11. visitor _____

12. resident _____

▶ **Write a Spelling Word for each clue.**

13. a small amount of time _____

14. a place that serves food _____

15. lawmakers, leaders, and judges _____

16. a mishap or misfortune _____

▶ **Write the following Spelling Words:** *servant, participant, statement, assistant.* **Use your best handwriting.**

17. _____   19. _____

18. _____   20. _____

SPELLING WORDS

1. absent
2. servant
3. present
4. instant
5. accident
6. assistant
7. current
8. moment
9. resident
10. ignorant
11. pleasant
12. distant
13. innocent
14. intelligent
15. restaurant
16. patient
17. government
18. statement
19. migrant
20. participant

Handwriting Tip: Be sure to make all your writing strokes smooth and flowing. Your letters and joining strokes should be smooth and even.

_____

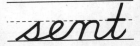

Harcourt

SPELLING WORDS

1. absent
2. servant
3. present
4. instant
5. accident
6. assistant
7. current
8. moment
9. resident
10. ignorant
11. pleasant
12. distant
13. innocent
14. intelligent
15. restaurant
16. patient
17. government
18. statement
19. migrant
20. participant

SPELLING STRATEGY

Mnemonics

You can make up a mnemonic clue to help you remember how to spell a word. For example, the silly sentence "An <u>ant</u> is ignor<u>ant</u>." can remind you to spell *ignorant* with *-ant*.

▶ Find the word in each pair that looks right. Then circle the one that looks wrong. Write the word that is correct.

1. ignorant   ignorent   _____

2. migrent   migrant   _____

3. innocint   innocent   _____

4. participant   participent   _____

5. present   presant   _____

6. servant   servent   _____

▶ Proofread the following newspaper headlines. Circle the misspelled Spelling Word in each one. Then write the word correctly.

Herald
Plane Accidant
Near Highway 80

7. _____

Gazette
Local Hero Enjoys
Instent Fame

10. _____

Journal
Oil at Currant Prices
Is a Bargain

8. _____

Tribune
Centerville Residant
Wins Award

11. _____

Times
Holiday Offers Pleasent
Weather for Swimming

9. _____

Express
Mayor Absant from
Ceremony

12. _____

Harcourt

Name _____

▶ **Fun with Words** Use Spelling Words to complete the word chain. Then write the words.

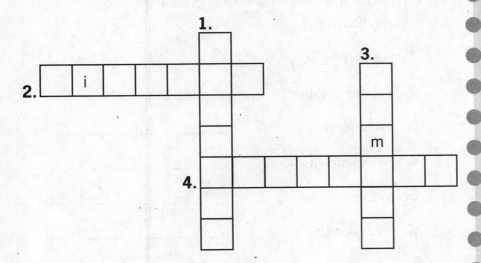

ACROSS

2. _____

4. _____

DOWN

1. _____

3. _____

▶ **Missing Vowels** Write the missing vowels to complete the Spelling Words. Then write the words.

7. ____nt____ll____g____nt   _____

8. st____t____m____nt   _____

9. r____st____ ____r____nt   _____

10. g____v____rnm____nt   _____

▶ **Rhyming Riddles** Answer the riddle by writing the Spelling Word that rhymes.

11. After you've waited for an hour at the doctor's office,

    you are an impatient _____.

12. If your lab helper is in another building, he or she is a

    distant _____.

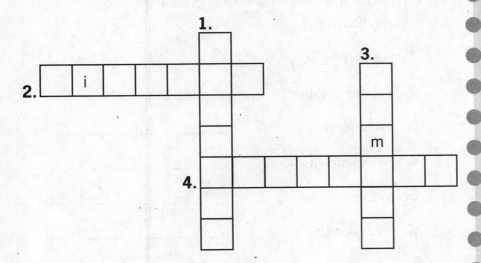

SPELLING WORDS

1. absent
2. servant
3. present
4. instant
5. accident
6. assistant
7. current
8. moment
9. resident
10. ignorant
11. pleasant
12. distant
13. innocent
14. intelligent
15. restaurant
16. patient
17. government
18. statement
19. migrant
20. participant

SPELLING WORDS

1. translation
2. laziness
3. population
4. invention
5. generation
6. examination
7. situation
8. operation
9. sickness
10. kindness
11. closeness
12. forgiveness
13. pollution
14. imagination
15. education
16. transportation
17. federation
18. subtraction
19. smallness
20. lateness

Handwriting Tip: Be sure to keep the joining stroke high when you write the letter *o*. Otherwise, the *o* could look like an *a*.

Name _____

Suffixes -*tion* and -*ness*

▶ **Write the Spelling Word that goes with each mini-definition.**

1. number of people _____

2. a set of conditions _____

3. a new device _____

4. investigation _____

5. contamination _____

6. process of learning _____

▶ **Write Spelling Words by adding a suffix to each related word. Make spelling changes if necessary.**

7. generate _____

8. lazy _____

9. imagine _____

10. kind _____

11. late _____

12. sick _____

13. small _____

14. subtract _____

15. translate _____

16. transport _____

▶ **Write the following Spelling Words:** *operation, closeness, forgiveness, federation.* **Use your best handwriting.**

17. _____ 19. _____

18. _____ 20. _____

Name_____

▶ Visualize the correct spelling of each misspelled word. Then write it correctly.

1. forgivness   _____

2. closness   _____

3. sicness   _____

4. subtracion   _____

▶ Proofread the following newspaper headlines. Circle the misspelled Spelling Word or Words in each. Then write the word correctly.

New Invension
Prevents Sicness

5. _____

6. _____

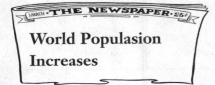

World Populasion
Increases

7. _____

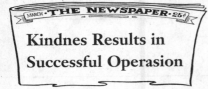

Kindnes Results in
Successful Operasion

8. _____

9. _____

▶ Write the Spelling Words that you find when you perform the math operations.

10. lazy − y + i + ness = _____

11. generator − tor + tion = _____

12. pollute − te + tion = _____

13. examine − e + a + tion = _____

14. federal − l + tion = _____

SPELLING WORDS

1. translation
2. laziness
3. population
4. invention
5. generation
6. examination
7. situation
8. operation
9. sickness
10. kindness
11. closeness
12. forgiveness
13. pollution
14. imagination
15. education
16. transportation
17. federation
18. subtraction
19. smallness
20. lateness

SPELLING
STRATEGY
Visualizing

Look at a word closely. Then look away and picture the word spelled correctly. Write the word.

Harcourt

SPELLING WORDS

1. translation
2. laziness
3. population
4. invention
5. generation
6. examination
7. situation
8. operation
9. sickness
10. kindness
11. closeness
12. forgiveness
13. pollution
14. imagination
15. education
16. transportation
17. federation
18. subtraction
19. smallness
20. lateness

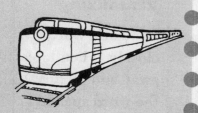

Name _____

▶ **Opposites** Mentally replace the little word in parentheses with its antonym. Then write the Spelling Word.

1. (out)vention _____

2. (stand)uation _____

3. (well)ness _____

4. (mean)ness _____

5. (open)ness _____

6. (mom)ulation _____

7. (large)ness _____

8. (early)ness _____

▶ **Fun with Words** Write a Spelling Word to fit in each word group.

9. dreams, creativity, pretending _____

10. classes, field trips, experiments _____

11. cars, trains, subways, jets _____

12. fractions, division, word problems _____

▶ **Mystery Vowels** For each ?, think of the missing vowel. Then write the Spelling Word.

13. tr?nsl?t??n _____

14. ?m?g?n?t??n _____

15. ?x?m?n?t??n _____

Harcourt

Practice Test

▶ Read each sentence. Find the correctly spelled word that completes the sentence. Fill in the oval next to the correct answer.

1. Write the title at the top of the _____.
   - ⬭ column
   - ⬭ colum
   - ⬭ collumn

2. Something is _____.
   - ⬭ rong
   - ⬭ wrone
   - ⬭ wrong

3. My sister is in _____.
   - ⬭ highschool
   - ⬭ hi-school
   - ⬭ high school

4. May I ride your _____?
   - ⬭ skateboard
   - ⬭ skate board
   - ⬭ skaitboard

5. We are _____ to go out.
   - ⬭ already
   - ⬭ all ready
   - ⬭ allready

6. You can mix it _____ you want.
   - ⬭ anyway
   - ⬭ any-way
   - ⬭ any way

7. Sue is a dental _____.
   - ⬭ asistant
   - ⬭ assistant
   - ⬭ assistent

8. A _____ groomed the horse.
   - ⬭ servant
   - ⬭ servent
   - ⬭ sirvant

9. _____ can become a habit.
   - ⬭ Laziness
   - ⬭ Lasiness
   - ⬭ Laisiness

10. The flu is a _____.
    - ⬭ sikness
    - ⬭ sickness
    - ⬭ sicknes

11. _____, the season when the leaves turn, is my favorite time of the year.
    - ⬭ Autumm
    - ⬭ Autum
    - ⬭ Autumn

12. Theater, dance, and music are three of the _____.
    - ⬭ fine arts
    - ⬭ finearts
    - ⬭ fine artes

Name _____

▶ **Read each sentence. If the underlined word is misspelled, fill in the oval next to the correct spelling. If the word is spelled correctly, fill in the third oval.**

1. The <u>yoake</u> of a bird's egg is yellow.
   ⬭ yolke   ⬭ yolk   ⬭ correct

2. I saw a <u>sowrd</u> at the museum.
   ⬭ sword   ⬭ swoard   ⬭ correct

3. Her sister plays in a <u>rock band</u>.
   ⬭ rock-band   ⬭ rokband   ⬭ correct

4. In the late 1800s, the <u>railroad</u> was the easiest way to travel across the country.
   ⬭ rail-road   ⬭ rail rode   ⬭ correct

5. <u>Its</u> time to go now.
   ⬭ It's   ⬭ Its'   ⬭ correct

6. Where is <u>you're</u> friend?
   ⬭ your'e   ⬭ your   ⬭ correct

7. We'll be ready in a <u>moment</u>.
   ⬭ momente   ⬭ momint   ⬭ correct

8. The <u>populasion</u> of our town is growing.
   ⬭ populateon   ⬭ population   ⬭ correct

9. The <u>presant</u> time is ten o'clock.
   ⬭ present   ⬭ presint   ⬭ correct

10. Give your brother your <u>forgiveness</u>.
    ⬭ forgivness   ⬭ forgivenes   ⬭ correct

11. I have never traveled to a <u>foreign</u> country.
    ⬭ forrun   ⬭ foriegn   ⬭ correct

12. Read this funny <u>comicstrip</u> about a mouse and a cat.
    ⬭ comick strip   ⬭ comic strip   ⬭ correct

Harcourt

Suffixes *-able* and *-less*

▶ **Write the Spelling Word that is the opposite of each given word.**

1. calm _____

2. tasty _____

3. meaningful _____

4. cautious _____

5. useful _____

6. capable _____

7. inexpensive _____

8. shallow _____

▶ **Write the Spelling Word that matches each clue.**

9. worthy _____

10. ready to use _____

11. competent _____

12. worth wishing for _____

13. trustworthy _____

14. snug and cozy _____

15. convincing _____

16. easily worked up _____

▶ **Write the following Spelling Words: *debatable*, *understandable*, *dampness*, *undeniable*. Use your best handwriting.**

17. _____   19. _____

18. _____   20. _____

SPELLING WORDS

1. capable
2. careless
3. desirable
4. admirable
5. restless
6. available
7. debatable
8. tasteless
9. helpless
10. senseless
11. priceless
12. useless
13. reliable
14. undeniable
15. excitable
16. believable
17. bottomless
18. comfortable
19. dampness
20. understandable

Handwriting Tip: Retrace, rather than loop, when you write the letter *d*, or the *d* could look like an *ol*.

d ol

SPELLING WORDS

1. capable
2. careless
3. desirable
4. admirable
5. restless
6. available
7. debatable
8. tasteless
9. helpless
10. senseless
11. priceless
12. useless
13. reliable
14. undeniable
15. excitable
16. believable
17. bottomless
18. comfortable
19. dampness
20. understandable

SPELLING STRATEGY

Comparing Spellings

If you are not sure how to spell a word, write it in different ways. Choose the spelling that looks correct, and check it in a dictionary.

▶ **Read each pair of words. Then circle the one that looks wrong. Write the word that is correct.**

1. tasteless   tastless   _____

2. debatible   debatable   _____

3. restless   restliss   _____

4. senselese   senseless   _____

5. usless   useless   _____

6. undeniabel   undeniable   _____

▶ **Read the job review. Circle the misspelled word in each set of parentheses. Write the words correctly on the lines below.**

Job Review Form

Name _____ Date _____
Job _____
Comments _____

- doesn't act (**helpless, helples**)

- is always (**availible, available**)

- shows (**admireable, admirable**) traits

- seems very (**capable, capible**)

- has many (**desireable, desirable**) qualities

- is always (**reliable, reliabal**)

7. _____   10. _____

8. _____   11. _____

9. _____   12. _____

Harcourt

Name _____

▶ **Pictures and Letters** Write the Spelling Word that fits each clue.

1. + able = _____

2. de + + able = _____

3. p + + less = _____

4. + eless = _____

5. + mirable = _____

6. + less = _____

7. under + + able = _____

▶ **Look Inside** Write the Spelling Word whose letters can be used to spell the four small words.

8. race, scar, real, lass _____

9. sip, crisp, pile, else _____

10. sir, bead, said, sale _____

11. amp, name, pass, seam _____

12. exit, cable, bleat, tax _____

13. loot, mess, boom, mole _____

14. veil, bell, live, blab _____

15. foam, roam, boat, more _____

SPELLING WORDS

1. capable
2. careless
3. desirable
4. admirable
5. restless
6. available
7. debatable
8. tasteless
9. helpless
10. senseless
11. priceless
12. useless
13. reliable
14. undeniable
15. excitable
16. believable
17. bottomless
18. comfortable
19. dampness
20. understandable

Harcourt

SPELLING WORDS

1. engineer
2. dentist
3. librarian
4. director
5. customer
6. pioneer
7. counselor
8. tourist
9. scientist
10. visitor
11. investigator
12. senator
13. astronomer
14. character
15. refrigerator
16. guardian
17. commander
18. physician
19. politician
20. leader

Handwriting Tip: Keep the joining stroke high when you join the letter *o* to other letters, or the *o* could look like an *a*.

_____

Suffixes *-eer*, *-ist*, *-ian*, *-or*, and *-er*

▶ Write the Spelling Word that names the person who does each job.

This is a person who:

1. runs for office _____
2. counsels _____
3. investigates _____
4. tours new places _____
5. has legal care of a child _____
6. conducts experiments _____
7. cares for the sick _____
8. fixes teeth _____

▶ Write the Spelling Word that names the person you might find in each place.

9. in a covered wagon _____
10. in the Senate _____
11. in a library _____
12. in a train locomotive _____
13. in a department store _____
14. in a novel, play, or story _____
15. at the front of a line _____
16. in command _____

▶ Write the following Spelling Words: *refrigerator, director, visitor, astronomer.* Use your best handwriting.

17. _____   19. _____

18. _____   20. _____

Harcourt

Name_____

▶ Read the Job Fair poster. Circle the eight misspelled words. Then write the words correctly.

> **JOB FAIR**
> MANY JOBS AVAILABLE.
> SIGN UP FOR AN INTERVIEW!
>
> train enginer   school libarian
> camp conseler   movie direkter
> private investigater   rocket sientest
> children's phisician   aerobics class leeder

1. _____

2. _____

3. _____

4. _____

5. _____

6. _____

7. _____

8. _____

▶ For each word below, write the Spelling Word that is related to the given word.

9. tour _____

10. command _____

11. counsel _____

12. custom _____

13. guard _____

14. library _____

SPELLING WORDS

1. engineer
2. dentist
3. librarian
4. director
5. customer
6. pioneer
7. counselor
8. tourist
9. scientist
10. visitor
11. investigator
12. senator
13. astronomer
14. character
15. refrigerator
16. guardian
17. commander
18. physician
19. politician
20. leader

SPELLING STRATEGY

Related Words

If you know how to spell a base word, then you can add prefixes and suffixes to help you spell words related to the base word.

Harcourt

SPELLING WORDS

1. engineer
2. dentist
3. librarian
4. director
5. customer
6. pioneer
7. counselor
8. tourist
9. scientist
10. visitor
11. investigator
12. senator
13. astronomer
14. character
15. refrigerator
16. guardian
17. commander
18. physician
19. politician
20. leader

▶ **Name Game** Write the Spelling Word that goes with each name.

1. Dr. Teeth _____

2. Mr. Guest _____

3. Prof. Experiment _____

4. Ms. Movie _____

5. Mrs. Train _____

6. Mr. Wilderness _____

7. Ms. Government _____

8. Dr. Telescope _____

▶ **Missing Letters** Each word has a missing letter. Identify that letter, and write the Spelling Word correctly.

9. gardian _____

10. refrigeratr _____

11. pioner _____

12. politican _____

13. caracter _____

14. sientist _____

15. physcian _____

16. comander _____

Harcourt

Name_____

Prefixes *non-*, *in-*, and *un-*

SPELLING WORDS

1. nontoxic
2. income
3. unknown
4. unusual
5. involved
6. unlike
7. inspector
8. unless
9. indeed
10. nonprofit
11. invisible
12. nonsense
13. incredible
14. uncomfortable
15. inconsistent
16. unfortunately
17. nonfiction
18. nonviolent
19. uncover
20. informal

▶ Write a Spelling Word that is the opposite of each given word by adding the prefix *non-*, *in-*, or *un-*.

1. profit _____

2. usual _____

3. toxic _____

4. visible _____

5. sense _____

6. known _____

7. credible _____

8. fortunately _____

9. cover _____

10. fiction _____

▶ Circle each misspelled word. Then write it correctly.

11. inconsistant   inconsistent   _____

12. inspector   inspecter   _____

13. involved   invalved   _____

14. informel   informal   _____

15. incume   income   _____

16. indead   indeed   _____

▶ Write the following Spelling Words: *nonviolent, uncomfortable, unlike, unless.* Use your best handwriting.

17. _____   19. _____

18. _____   20. _____

Handwriting Tip: Be sure that the letter *l* touches the top line. Otherwise, an *l* could look like an *i*.

Harcourt

SPELLING WORDS

1. nontoxic
2. income
3. unknown
4. unusual
5. involved
6. unlike
7. inspector
8. unless
9. indeed
10. nonprofit
11. invisible
12. nonsense
13. incredible
14. uncomfortable
15. inconsistent
16. unfortunately
17. nonfiction
18. nonviolent
19. uncover
20. informal

SPELLING STRATEGY

Dictionary Skills

The guide words at the top of each dictionary page help you find a word.

▶ Write each Spelling Word under the guide words that could appear on its page in a dictionary. Make sure each list is in alphabetical order.

income	nonprofit	nonsense	nonfiction
involved	invisible	nontoxic	inconsistent

inactive—inward

1. _____
2. _____
3. _____
4. _____

nominate—normal

5. _____
6. _____
7. _____
8. _____

▶ Read the letter of complaint. Circle the seven misspelled words. Then write the words correctly.

Dear Inspecter Sharpnose,

I am writing to complain about an unusule smell that is in my house. It seems to be coming from an unnown source. I hope that it is nontoxik. Inded, I am very concerned about it. Unles you can help me, I might have to move out. The smell is unlik anything I have ever smelled before!

Most sincerely,
James Strong

9. _____   13. _____

10. _____   14. _____

11. _____   15. _____

12. _____

Harcourt

Name_____

▶ **Use the Clues** Write the Spelling Word that fits each clue.

word with a final
double consonant   1. _____

word with long *e* sound   2. _____

word with /yoo/   3. _____

word with "silent" letter *k*   4. _____

two words with long   5.–6. _____
i sound
                             _____

three words that end   7.–9. _____
with *ble*
                             _____

                             _____

▶ **Mystery Vowels** For each ?, think of the missing vowel. Then write the Spelling Word.

10. ?nf?rm?l   _____

11. ?nf?rt?n?t?l?   _____

12. ?nc?v?r   _____

13. ?nsp?ct?r   _____

▶ **Fun with Words** Write the Spelling Word that fits inside each word shape.

14.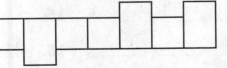

15.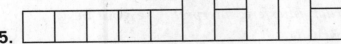

16.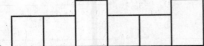

1. nontoxic
2. income
3. unknown
4. unusual
5. involved
6. unlike
7. inspector
8. unless
9. indeed
10. nonprofit
11. invisible
12. nonsense
13. incredible
14. uncomfortable
15. inconsistent
16. unfortunately
17. nonfiction
18. nonviolent
19. uncover
20. informal

Harcourt

SPELLING WORDS

1. remove
2. interview
3. repeat
4. interrupt
5. respect
6. interfere
7. represent
8. relocate
9. international
10. review
11. interpret
12. interstate
13. remarkable
14. intermediate
15. intersection
16. recommend
17. interject
18. intervene
19. resource
20. remained

Prefixes re- and inter-

▶ **Write the Spelling Word that matches each word or phrase.**

1. stayed _____

2. source of supply _____

3. noteworthy _____

4. between states _____

5. honor _____

6. take away _____

7. study again _____

8. stand for _____

9. move to a
   new location _____

10. say again _____

11. suggest _____

12. involving two or
    more countries _____

▶ **Write the Spelling Words in alphabetical order.**

| intersection   interject   intervene   intermediate |

13. _____ 15. _____

14. _____ 16. _____

▶ **Write the following Spelling Words: *interview,
interrupt, interfere, interpret.* Use your best
handwriting.**

17. _____ 19. _____

18. _____ 20. _____

Handwriting Tip: Do not loop the letter *i*. It could easily be mistaken for an *e*.

_____

SPELLING PRACTICE BOOK **LESSON 19**

Harcourt

Name _____

▶ **Read the interview. Circle the eight misspelled words.
Write them correctly.**

Question: Is this your first intervuw?
Answer: Yes. Is it okay if I remoove my coat?

Question: Do you plan to relokate if you get the job?
Answer: No, I need to rispekt my family's wishes.

Question: What company do you now reprezent?
Answer: I work for a large internasional firm.

Question: How would you interprit the recent developments?
Answer: I would have to reveiw them before I let you know.

1. _____ 5. _____

2. _____ 6. _____

3. _____ 7. _____

4. _____ 8. _____

▶ **Work with a partner to circle each misspelled word.
Then write it correctly.**

9. interjecct   interject   _____

10. remarkable   remarkible   _____

11. recommend   reccomend   _____

12. interupt   interrupt   _____

13. intersection   intersecshion _____

14. resorce   resource   _____

SPELLING WORDS

1. remove
2. interview
3. repeat
4. interrupt
5. respect
6. interfere
7. represent
8. relocate
9. international
10. review
11. interpret
12. interstate
13. remarkable
14. intermediate
15. intersection
16. recommend
17. interject
18. intervene
19. resource
20. remained

SPELLING STRATEGY

Working Together

When you proofread, work with a partner to find misspelled words.

SPELLING WORDS

1. remove
2. interview
3. repeat
4. interrupt
5. respect
6. interfere
7. represent
8. relocate
9. international
10. review
11. interpret
12. interstate
13. remarkable
14. intermediate
15. intersection
16. recommend
17. interject
18. intervene
19. resource
20. remained

▶ **Hidden Words** Circle eleven Spelling Words. Then write the words.

```
i n t e r s t a t e r x o
r e m o v e r e s p e c t
e r e v i e w f m r p f a
p i n t e r r u p t r u n
e s i n t e r f e r e o w
a b o x s u e k i m s t m
t i n t e r v i e w e m h
q r e l o c a t e s n j a
i n t e r p r e t r t a r
```

1. _____   7. _____

2. _____   8. _____

3. _____   9. _____

4. _____   10. _____

5. _____   11. _____

6. _____

▶ **Missing Letters** Each word has a missing letter. Identify that letter, and write the Spelling Word correctly.

12. remaned   _____

13. interven   _____

14. resorce   _____

15. intermedate _____

16. intersetion _____

17. internatinal _____

18. intrstate   _____

Harcourt

Prefixes *dis-* and *de-*

▶ **Write the Spelling Word that matches each word or words.**

1. to take away _____

2. protection _____

3. to annoy _____

4. to insist _____

5. to talk over _____

6. to build _____

7. sickness _____

8. not meeting expectations _____

9. to become invisible _____

10. feeling low on hope _____

11. a loss _____

▶ **Write the Spelling Word that is the opposite of the given word.**

12. admitted _____

13. mark-up _____

14. generalizations _____

15. lazy _____

16. happy _____

Handwriting Tip: Be sure to close the letter *d* and not to loop it. Otherwise, the *d* could look like a *cl*.

_____ *d cl*

▶ **Write the following Spelling Words: *disconnect*, *descent*, *disadvantage*, *demonstrated*. Use your best handwriting.**

17. _____   19. _____

18. _____   20. _____

Harcourt

SPELLING WORDS

1. discuss
2. deduct
3. dismissed
4. develop
5. disease
6. discount
7. disturb
8. details
9. demand
10. determined
11. depressed
12. defense
13. disappointing
14. discouraged
15. disadvantage
16. demonstrated
17. defeat
18. descent
19. disappear
20. disconnect

SPELLING STRATEGY

Word Shapes

Drawing the shape of a word can help you remember how to spell it.

▶ Read the following list. Circle the nine misspelled words. Then write the words correctly.

Things to Do

1. Develope film.

2. Go to discont store.

3. Disscus trip detals with travel agent.

4. Dedukt money from bank account.

5. Buy "Do not desturb" sign.

6. Demaned an answer from Rob.

7. Buy heart dizeaze pills for dog.

8. Disconect second phone line.

_____
_____
_____
_____
_____
_____
_____
_____

▶ Inside each word shape, write the Spelling Word that fits.

9.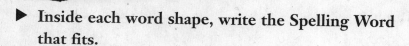

10.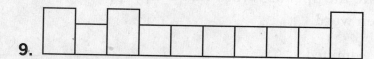

11.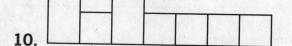

12.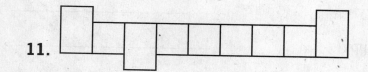

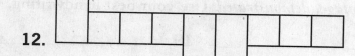

Name_____

▶ **Hidden Words** Write the Spelling Words that contain these smaller words.

1. miss _____

2. tail _____

3. disc _____

4. ease _____

5. man _____

6. count _____

7. eve _____

8. pear _____

9. point _____

10. mine _____

11. cent _____

12. rate _____

13. press _____

14. connect _____

15. courage _____

▶ **Word Scramble** Unscramble each group of letters to write a Spelling Word.

16. aedfet _____

17. ensdfee _____

18. ugaerdsocid _____

19. brustid _____

20. vdangetsidaa _____

Harcourt

Practice Test

▶ **Read each group of words. Fill in the letter of the word that is spelled correctly.**

1
(A) admirable
(B) admireable
(C) admerable
(D) admirible

2
(F) customor
(G) costomer
(H) custamer
(J) customer

3
(A) torist
(B) turist
(C) tourist
(D) taurist

4
(F) invizible
(G) unvisible
(H) invisible
(J) invisable

5
(A) useless
(B) yousles
(C) usles
(D) useles

6
(F) inusual
(G) unusual
(H) unuzual
(J) unutual

7
(A) interupt
(B) interrupt
(C) interrupped
(D) inteript

8
(F) review
(G) revew
(H) reveiw
(J) reveuw

9
(A) dimand
(B) demande
(C) demend
(D) demand

10
(F) disese
(G) disease
(H) diseas
(J) diseaze

11
(A) reliabel
(B) reliabal
(C) relyable
(D) reliable

12
(F) uncomfortable
(G) uncomfortabel
(H) unconfortable
(J) unconfortible

Harcourt

► **Read each sentence. Decide whether the underlined word is spelled correctly or incorrectly. Fill in the oval beside the answer you have chosen.**

1. I liked reading about the <u>details</u> of the story.
   ⬭ correct   ⬭ incorrect

2. My family will <u>discuss</u> our vacation plans.
   ⬭ correct   ⬭ incorrect

3. It is not fun to be around a <u>careles</u> person.
   ⬭ correct   ⬭ incorrect

4. I am <u>available</u> to baby-sit on Wednesday.
   ⬭ correct   ⬭ incorrect

5. She saw the <u>dentest</u> yesterday.
   ⬭ correct   ⬭ incorrect

6. The <u>librarian</u> can suggest a book.
   ⬭ correct   ⬭ incorrect

7. I earn my <u>income</u> by walking dogs.
   ⬭ correct   ⬭ incorrect

8. You won't know <u>unles</u> you ask.
   ⬭ correct   ⬭ incorrect

9. <u>Respekt</u> your parents.
   ⬭ correct   ⬭ incorrect

10. I watched the <u>interview</u> on television.
    ⬭ correct   ⬭ incorrect

11. Young children are often rather <u>excitable</u>.
    ⬭ correct   ⬭ incorrect

12. Please don't leave the <u>refrigerater</u> door standing open!
    ⬭ correct   ⬭ incorrect

SPELLING WORDS

1. prevent
2. program
3. predict
4. project
5. pretend
6. process
7. prefer
8. promise
9. previous
10. protect
11. property
12. propose
13. precede
14. proceed
15. pronunciation
16. professional
17. pretest
18. preview
19. proclaim
20. progress

Prefixes *pre-* and *pro-*

▶ Read the campaign speech. Mentally fill in *pre-* or *pro-* to write Spelling Words on the lines.

The **(1)** _____ (cess) of elections involves candidates and voters. The candidates must do more than

(2) _____ (mise) a longer recess. They must

(3) _____ (pose) ideas after careful thought

and think about **(4)** _____ (vious) plans.

Which **(5)** _____ (gram) worked well? Which

(6) _____ (ject) was a mistake? Which will

(7) _____ (tect) students'

(8) _____ (perty) the best and

(9) _____ (vent) a loss of student morale?
The voters must decide which candidate they **(10)**

_____ (fer) and **(11)** _____ (dict)

who will be the best leader. Don't **(12)** _____
(tend) that elections are unimportant.

▶ Write the Spelling Words in alphabetical order.

| proclaim | professional | proceed | progress |

13. _____   15. _____

14. _____   16. _____

▶ Write the following Spelling Words: *precede, preview, pretest, pronunciation.* Use your best handwriting.

17. _____   19. _____

18. _____   20. _____

Handwriting Tip: Remember that tall letters should touch the top and the bottom line, and most short letters should touch the imaginary midline and the bottom line.

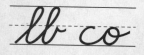

SPELLING PRACTICE BOOK

LESSON 21

Name _____

▶ Read the list of entries in the Science Fair competition. Circle the seven misspelled words. Then write the words correctly.

VOTE FOR THE
FIRST-PRIZE PROJECK

Ways to Proteck Your Properte
How to Provent Wildfires
Prociss for Making Maple Syrup
How to Prodict the Weather
Five-Step Pregram for Good Health

1. _____   5. _____

2. _____   6. _____

3. _____   7. _____

4. _____

▶ Write the Spelling Word that is the opposite of each given word.

8. follow   _____

9. amateur   _____

10. next   _____

11. posttest   _____

12. dislike   _____

▶ Write the Spelling Word that matches each mini-definition.

13. to make believe   _____

14. vow   _____

15. a sign of advancement _____

SPELLING WORDS

1. prevent
2. program
3. predict
4. project
5. pretend
6. process
7. prefer
8. promise
9. previous
10. protect
11. property
12. propose
13. precede
14. proceed
15. pronunciation
16. professional
17. pretest
18. preview
19. proclaim
20. progress

SPELLING STRATEGY

Classifying Errors

Start a spelling journal to help you keep track of the kinds of spelling errors you make most often.

Harcourt

SPELLING WORDS

1. prevent
2. program
3. predict
4. project
5. pretend
6. process
7. prefer
8. promise
9. previous
10. protect
11. property
12. propose
13. precede
14. proceed
15. pronunciation
16. professional
17. pretest
18. preview
19. proclaim
20. progress

▶ **Word Parts** Using the key below, change the numbers into word parts. Then write the Spelling Word.

| 1 = pre | 3 = vent | 5 = mise | 7 = pose |
| 2 = pro | 4 = dict | 6 = tect | 8 = ject |

1. 1 + 3 = _____   4. 2 + 8 = _____

2. 2 + 5 = _____   5. 2 + 7 = _____

3. 1 + 4 = _____   6. 2 + 6 = _____

▶ **Hidden Words** Starting with the second letter of each word, cross out every other letter. Write the remaining letters. You will write a Spelling Word.

7. p l r v e x t y e t n v d s _____

8. p d r g e i v m i c o j u p s d _____

9. p j r s o t g m r o a y m b _____

10. p r r e o s c p e e e c d t _____

▶ **Missing Vowels** Write the Spelling Words by filling in the missing vowels.

11. prcss _____

12. prvnt _____

13. prclm _____

14. prnnctn _____

15. prvw _____

SPELLING PRACTICE BOOK   **LESSON 21**

Harcourt

Name_____

VCCV Words

▶ **Write the Spelling Word that matches each clue.**

1. This follows lightning. _____

2. Smoke goes up this. _____

3. another word for *maybe* _____

4. When you try hard,
   you make an _____. _____

5. the opposite of ugly _____

6. You sleep under this. _____

7. all of it _____

8. twisted, salted bread _____

9. a kind of help _____

10. "My _____ Americans . . ." _____

11. start fighting _____

12. a topic _____

▶ **Write a Spelling Word to complete each sentence.**

13. Has the medicine taken _____ yet?

14. Yoshi got a scholarship to _____.

15. Rest your head on the _____.

16. You need to eat, drink, and breathe to _____.

▶ **Write the following Spelling Words:** *tunnel, suspended, challenge, hunger.* **Use your best handwriting.**

17. _____   19. _____

18. _____   20. _____

SPELLING WORDS

1. pretty
2. service
3. thunder
4. blanket
5. effort
6. fellow
7. subject
8. perhaps
9. attack
10. entire
11. chimney
12. tunnel
13. effect
14. suspended
15. challenge
16. pretzel
17. survive
18. pillow
19. hunger
20. college

Handwriting Tip: Use only one overcurve joining stroke before forming the letter *n*. Otherwise, the *n* could look like an *m*.

_____

m m

Harcourt

SPELLING WORDS

1. pretty
2. service
3. thunder
4. blanket
5. effort
6. fellow
7. subject
8. perhaps
9. attack
10. entire
11. chimney
12. tunnel
13. effect
14. suspended
15. challenge
16. pretzel
17. survive
18. pillow
19. hunger
20. college

SPELLING STRATEGY

Listening Carefully

Think of the spelling patterns that can make the sounds in a word.

▶ **Read the diary entry. Circle the eight misspelled words. Then write the words correctly.**

Dear Diary,

   The thundir really scared me. It lasted the intire night. I pulled my blankut over my head, hoping to shut out some of the noise. It felt as though the whole cabin were shaking. I thought the chimnie was going to fall down. It was prety awful, but I made an efort to stay calm. I didn't want to appear nervous in front of my felow campers. If there had been an underground tunnle, however, I would have crawled into it!

1. _____ 5. _____

2. _____ 6. _____

3. _____ 7. _____

4. _____ 8. _____

▶ **Circle the misspelled word in each pair. Then write the correctly spelled word, and draw a line (|) between its syllables.**

9. sevice   service   _____

10. subject   subjict   _____

11. perhips   perhaps   _____

12. colledge   college   _____

13. hunger   hungur   _____

14. pretzel   pretzle   _____

15. servive   survive   _____

16. atack   attack   _____

Harcourt

Name_____

▶ **Hidden Words** Write the Spelling Words that contain these smaller words.

1. tack _____

2. blank _____

3. under _____

4. tire _____

5. spend _____

6. ill _____

7. hall _____

8. him _____

9. fell _____

10. vice _____

▶ **Mix and Match** Rearrange the four syllables to write two Spelling Words.

pret	fort	ef	ty
fel	tun	low	nel
der	thun	ject	sub
ef	vive	sur	fect

11. _____

12. _____

13. _____

14. _____

15. _____

16. _____

17. _____

18. _____

SPELLING WORDS

1. pretty
2. service
3. thunder
4. blanket
5. effort
6. fellow
7. subject
8. perhaps
9. attack
10. entire
11. chimney
12. tunnel
13. effect
14. suspended
15. challenge
16. pretzel
17. survive
18. pillow
19. hunger
20. college

Harcourt

SPELLING WORDS

1. wondering
2. fastened
3. permitting
4. controlled
5. listening
6. regretted
7. suffered
8. admitted
9. referred
10. bothered
11. submitted
12. whispered
13. transferred
14. occurring
15. canceled
16. developing
17. scrubbing
18. upsetting
19. wondered
20. quarreled

Handwriting Tip: Remember to slant your letters in the same direction, keep your paper in the proper position, and hold your pencil correctly.

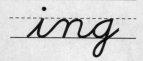

More Words with -ed or -ing

▶ Write the Spelling Word that is the opposite of each given word.

1. ignoring   _____

2. shouted   _____

3. denied   _____

4. thrived   _____

5. chaotic   _____

6. pleasing   _____

7. unclasped   _____

8. preventing   _____

▶ Write the Spelling Word for each clue.

9. felt sorry about   _____

10. handed in   _____

11. argued   _____

12. cleaning thoroughly   _____

13. thought about   _____

14. removed from the schedule _____

15. happening   _____

16. changing   _____

▶ Write the following Spelling Words: *referred, wondering, transferred, bothered.* Use your best handwriting.

17. _____   19. _____

18. _____   20. _____

Harcourt

Name _____

▶ **Read the sentences. Circle the eight misspelled words. Then write the words correctly.**

Stacy admitted that she had broken the plate.

They fasened a rope to the tree.

He is wundering what to do with his birthday money.

We regreted not being able to go to the party.

The animal trainer controled the tigers.

My teacher reffered me to a book in the library.

The game was cansseled due to rain.

How upseting it is to hear that you are moving!

1. _____   5. _____

2. _____   6. _____

3. _____   7. _____

4. _____   8. _____

▶ **Write the Spelling Word that best completes each of these sentences.**

9. Many people _____ during the harsh, cold winter.

10. I _____ the secret in Ashley's ear.

11. Luisa _____ her geography report on time.

12. After I yelled at my brother, I _____ it.

13. A mosquito _____ me last night and kept me awake.

14. We like to ride in the car, _____ to the radio.

15. My parents are _____ me to see that movie.

SPELLING WORDS

1. wondering
2. fastened
3. permitting
4. controlled
5. listening
6. regretted
7. suffered
8. admitted
9. referred
10. bothered
11. submitted
12. whispered
13. transferred
14. occurring
15. canceled
16. developing
17. scrubbing
18. upsetting
19. wondered
20. quarreled

SPELLING STRATEGY

Reading Backward

To proofread, start with the last word and end with the first.

Harcourt

SPELLING WORDS

1. wondering
2. fastened
3. permitting
4. controlled
5. listening
6. regretted
7. suffered
8. admitted
9. referred
10. bothered
11. submitted
12. whispered
13. transferred
14. occurring
15. canceled
16. developing
17. scrubbing
18. upsetting
19. wondered
20. quarreled

▶ **Double or Nothing** Add *-ed* to each word. Double a letter if necessary. Write the Spelling Word.

1. admit _____

2. whisper _____

3. fasten _____

4. suffer _____

5. refer _____

6. transfer _____

7. quarrel _____

8. wonder _____

▶ **Missing Vowels** Write the missing vowels to complete the Spelling Words. Then write the words.

9. _____cc_____rr_____ng

   _____

10. d_____v_____l_____p_____ng

    _____

11. scr_____bb_____ng

    _____

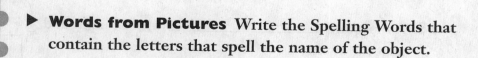

12. q_____ _____rr_____l_____d

    _____

▶ **Words from Pictures** Write the Spelling Words that contain the letters that spell the name of the object.

13. _____

14. _____

15. _____

Harcourt

Name_____

VCCCV Words

SPELLING WORDS

▶ **Write the Spelling Word that is the opposite of each given word.**

1. simple _____

2. worsen _____

3. expand _____

4. add _____

5. belief _____

6. agreement _____

7. compliment _____

8. attract _____

9. not enough _____

10. destruction _____

11. dinner party _____

12. soup _____

SPELLING WORDS

1. subtract
2. distract
3. contract
4. complex
5. distrust
6. extra
7. improve
8. instead
9. Congress
10. English
11. conflict
12. exchange
13. pumpkin
14. sandwich
15. Christmas
16. construction
17. luncheon
18. complaint
19. transform
20. although

▶ **Write a Spelling Word to complete each sentence.**

13. _____ is a language.

14. Let's carve the _____ .

15. The travelers had to _____ their money for U.S. dollars.

16. Fresh paint will _____ the bedroom.

▶ **Write the following Spelling Words: *although*, *Christmas*, *Congress*, *instead*. Use your best handwriting.**

17. _____

18. _____

19. _____

20. _____

Handwriting Tip: Be sure that the bottom parts of your uppercase and lowercase letters sit evenly on the bottom line.

Harcourt

Name _____

▶ **Read the book titles. Circle the misspelled word in each title. Then write the words correctly.**

The History of the United States Congriss

1. _____

Emprove Your Fitness

2. _____

The Development of the Inglish Language

3. _____

Comflict Between Nations

4. _____

Peace Unstead of War

5. _____

Comeplex World Politics

6. _____

Diztrust Among Enemies

7. _____

How to Make Exstra Money

8. _____

Christmass Cooking and Baking

9. _____

▶ **With a partner, take turns circling misspelled words and writing them correctly.**

10. contract   condract   _____

11. ecshange   exchange   _____

12. subetract   subtract   _____

13. distract   distrackt   _____

14. although   altho   _____

15. lunchin   luncheon   _____

Name_____

▶ **Word Math** Add and subtract syllables to form Spelling Words.

1. attract − at + sub = _____

2. distract − dis + con = _____

3. subtract − sub + dis = _____

4. improvement − ment = _____

5. steady + in − y = _____

6. formation − ation + trans = _____

7. plaintive − ive + com = _____

▶ **Remove Letters** In each misspelled word, cross out the letter that does not belong. Then write the Spelling Word correctly.

8. construcktion _____

9. conflickt _____

10. Engelish _____

11. exstra _____

12. allthough _____

13. Coungress _____

▶ **Fun with Words** Write the Spelling Word that names each picture.

14. _____   15. _____

SPELLING WORDS
1. subtract
2. distract
3. contract
4. complex
5. distrust
6. extra
7. improve
8. instead
9. Congress
10. English
11. conflict
12. exchange
13. pumpkin
14. sandwich
15. Christmas
16. construction
17. luncheon
18. complaint
19. transform
20. although

Harcourt

SPELLING WORDS

1. slogan
2. radar
3. minutes
4. honest
5. second
6. virus
7. shadow
8. humor
9. salad
10. eleven
11. closet
12. model
13. volcano
14. private
15. balance
16. radio
17. basis
18. decent
19. fanatic
20. novel

Handwriting Tip: Be sure to keep the joining stroke high on the letter *o*. Otherwise, the *o* could look like an *a*.

_____

VCV Words

▶ **Write the Spelling Word that fits each clue.**

1. There are sixty of these in an hour. _____

2. It's between first and third. _____

3. It's between ten and twelve. _____

4. where clothes are kept _____

5. This causes disease. _____

6. It's made with lettuce. _____

7. In late afternoon, this is long. _____

8. a motto _____

9. This device plays music. _____

▶ **Write a Spelling Word to complete each sentence.**

10. Airports use _____ to monitor the planes.

11. The _____ posed for the photographer.

12. The gymnast has excellent _____.

13. You will have homework on a regular _____.

14. The food isn't great, but it's _____.

15. Derek is a baseball _____.

16. I write my _____ thoughts in a diary.

▶ **Write the following Spelling Words:** *volcano, honest, novel, humor.* **Use your best handwriting.**

17. _____   19. _____

18. _____   20. _____

Harcourt

Name_____

▶ **Read the schedule. Circle the five misspelled words. Then write the words correctly.**

Sunday: Make tuna **(salid, salad)** for picnic.

1. _____

Monday: Clean out supply **(closet, closset)**.

2. _____

Tuesday: Get a shot to prevent flu **(viras, virus)**.

3. _____

Wednesday: Do report on "**(Honist, Honest)** Abe."

4. _____

Saturday: Read a good mystery **(novel, novle)**.

5. _____

▶ **For each word pair, circle the word that looks wrong. Write the word that is correct.**

6. minutes	minites	_____
7. sekond	second	_____
8. humor	humer	_____
9. raedar	radar	_____
10. honist	honest	_____

▶ **Write the Spelling Word that names each picture.**

11. **11** _____

12. _____

13. _____

SPELLING WORDS

1. slogan
2. radar
3. minutes
4. honest
5. second
6. virus
7. shadow
8. humor
9. salad
10. eleven
11. closet
12. model
13. volcano
14. private
15. balance
16. radio
17. basis
18. decent
19. fanatic
20. novel

SPELLING STRATEGY

Comparing Spellings

If you don't remember how to spell a word, write it using different spellings. Compare the spellings, and choose the one that looks right. Then check the spelling in a dictionary.

Harcourt

SPELLING WORDS

1. slogan
2. radar
3. minutes
4. honest
5. second
6. virus
7. shadow
8. humor
9. salad
10. eleven
11. closet
12. model
13. volcano
14. private
15. balance
16. radio
17. basis
18. decent
19. fanatic
20. novel

Name _____

▶ **Letter Leapfrog** In each item that follows, the letters of two Spelling Words alternate. Write both Spelling Words. Hint: The letters for each word are in the correct order.

smaoldaedl   1. _____   2. _____

cslhoasdeotw   3. _____   4. _____

rbaadsiios   5. _____   6. _____

▶ **Missing Consonants** Supply the missing consonants. Then write the Spelling Word.

7. ____ o ____ e ____   _____

8. ____ ____ a ____ o ____   _____

9. ____ ____ i ____ a ____ e   _____

10. ____ a ____ a ____ i ____   _____

11. ____ e ____ e ____   _____

▶ **What Do You See?** Write the Spelling Words that name things included in the picture.

12. _____   15. _____

13. _____   16. _____

14. _____

Harcourt

Practice Test

▶ **Read each sentence. Find the correctly spelled word that completes the sentence. Fill in the oval next to the correct answer.**

1. I _____ that I'll be home early.
   - ⬭ promis
   - ⬭ promise
   - ⬭ pramis

2. Who can _____ what will happen next?
   - ⬭ predict
   - ⬭ predicte
   - ⬭ predect

3. This _____ will keep you warm.
   - ⬭ blankit
   - ⬭ blankete
   - ⬭ blanket

4. Sometimes _____ is very loud.
   - ⬭ thundre
   - ⬭ thunder
   - ⬭ thonder

5. The children _____ in the back seat.
   - ⬭ whistperd
   - ⬭ whisperde
   - ⬭ whispered

6. We were _____ who was at the door.
   - ⬭ wondering
   - ⬭ wondring
   - ⬭ wundering

7. Friends often _____ phone numbers.
   - ⬭ exchang
   - ⬭ exchainge
   - ⬭ exchange

8. The pizza has _____ cheese.
   - ⬭ extra
   - ⬭ estra
   - ⬭ egstra

9. Jon's campaign _____ is funny.
   - ⬭ sloagen
   - ⬭ slogen
   - ⬭ slogan

10. My sister is a _____ about crossword puzzles.
    - ⬭ fenatic
    - ⬭ fenatick
    - ⬭ fanatic

11. Are we making _____ toward our goal?
    - ⬭ progress
    - ⬭ progriss
    - ⬭ porgress

12. My sister is a senior in _____ .
    - ⬭ collage
    - ⬭ collidge
    - ⬭ college

Harcourt

Name_____

▶ **Read each sentence. Choose the word in parentheses that is spelled correctly. Fill in the oval beneath that word.**

1. The **(project, praject)** is taking a long time.
   ⬭   ⬭

2. These knee pads will **(protecte, protect)** his knees.
   ⬭   ⬭

3. The mole made a **(tunnle, tunnel)** under the ground.
   ⬭   ⬭

4. Math is her favorite **(subject, subjecked)**.
   ⬭   ⬭

5. Susan **(admited, admitted)** that she was confused.
   ⬭   ⬭

6. The barking dog **(bothered, bathered)** all the neighbors.
   ⬭   ⬭

7. Please sign the **(contrac, contract)**.
   ⬭   ⬭

8. The first language I learned was **(English, engllish)**.
   ⬭   ⬭

9. Sixty **(minutes, minits)** are in an hour.
   ⬭   ⬭

10. Hang your coat in the **(closit, closet)**.
    ⬭   ⬭

11. The Introduction should **(precede, preceed)** Chapter One.
    ⬭   ⬭

12. This **(pretzel, pretzle)** is too salty for me.
    ⬭   ⬭

13. The children **(quarraled, quarreled)** over the toy.
    ⬭   ⬭

14. **(Altho, Although)** they were tired, the runners ran on.
    ⬭   ⬭

Harcourt

VV Words

▶ **Write the Spelling Word that goes with each mini-definition.**

1. a hardship _____

2. the center of a cell or atom _____

3. mean-spirited _____

4. aggressive; wanting to fight _____

5. to destroy _____

6. victory _____

7. Native American _____

8. making very little noise _____

9. to have an effect on; change _____

10. rhyming verse _____

11. an untruthful person _____

12. energy in liquid form _____

▶ **Write the Spelling Word that best completes each analogy.**

13. *Library* is to *books* as _____ is to *paintings*.

14. *School* is to *students* as _____ is to *actors*.

15. *Hammer* is to *tool* as _____ is to *instrument*.

16. *Fish* is to *brook* as _____ is to *tree*.

▶ **Write the following Spelling Words: *fluid, diet, leotard, dial.* Use your best handwriting.**

17. _____   19. _____

18. _____   20. _____

SPELLING WORDS

1. quiet
2. trial
3. fuel
4. poem
5. diet
6. nucleus
7. cruel
8. Indian
9. fluid
10. violin
11. museum
12. dial
13. ruin
14. influence
15. triumph
16. violent
17. theater
18. liar
19. leotard
20. koala

Handwriting Tip: Be sure to close the letter *d*, but be careful not to loop it. Otherwise, the *d* could look like *el*.

d el

Harcourt

SPELLING WORDS

1. quiet
2. trial
3. fuel
4. poem
5. diet
6. nucleus
7. cruel
8. Indian
9. fluid
10. violin
11. museum
12. dial
13. ruin
14. influence
15. triumph
16. violent
17. theater
18. liar
19. leotard
20. koala

SPELLING STRATEGY

Adjoining Vowel Sounds

Pronounce words slowly to yourself. Listen for the vowel sounds to be sure that you have written the vowels in the correct order.

▶ **Circle the misspelled word in each New Year's resolution. Then write the words correctly.**

My New Year's Resolutions

1. have some (**quieit, quiet**) time every day _____

2. eat a balanced (**diet, deit**) _____

3. practice the (**vialin, violin**) _____

4. visit a (**musuem, museum**) _____

5. write a (**poem, peom**) a week _____

6. go to the (**theater, thaeter**) once or twice _____

▶ **Read the list of museum exhibits. Circle the misspelled word in each title. Then write the words correctly.**

7. The History of the Voilin _____

8. Telling Time with a Sun Dail _____

9. The Court Trail of the Century _____

10. Creul Winter Storms _____

11. Sources of Feul _____

12. The Nuclues of the Cell _____

▶ **Circle the misspelled words. Then write them correctly.**

13. leatard   leotard _____

14. koala   koloa _____

15. fluid   flued _____

SPELLING PRACTICE BOOK   **LESSON 26**

Name _____

► **Working with Meaning** Write the Spelling Word that is the opposite of each clue.

1. to construct; build up   _____

2. an honest person   _____

3. surrender   _____

4. to have no effect on   _____

5. calm and peaceful   _____

► **Fun with Words** Use Spelling Words to complete the puzzle. Then write the words.

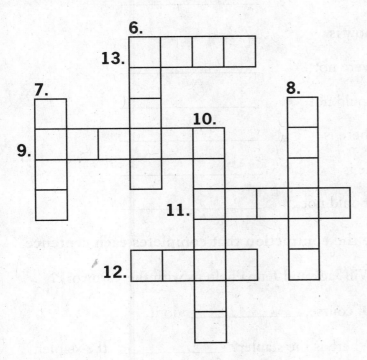

ACROSS

9. the name of an ocean

11. the opposite of *kind*

12. a form of writing

13. gasoline

DOWN

6. what flows easily

7. a way to lose weight

8. a place with exhibits

10. a central part

SPELLING WORDS

1. quiet
2. trial
3. fuel
4. poem
5. diet
6. nucleus
7. cruel
8. Indian
9. fluid
10. violin
11. museum
12. dial
13. ruin
14. influence
15. triumph
16. violent
17. theater
18. liar
19. leotard
20. koala

Harcourt

SPELLING WORDS

1. he's
2. couldn't
3. she'll
4. doesn't
5. we'd
6. that's
7. hadn't
8. shouldn't
9. how's
10. weren't
11. there's
12. wouldn't
13. what's
14. where's
15. aren't
16. here's
17. they'll
18. we'll
19. you'd
20. he'd

Handwriting Tip: Be careful not to join the letters before and after the apostrophe in a contraction.

Name _____

Contractions

▶ Write the Spelling Word that is the contraction of the two words.

1. we had _____

2. had not _____

3. that is _____

4. does not _____

5. would not _____

6. she will _____

7. how is _____

8. were not _____

9. could not _____

10. there is _____

11. he is _____

12. should not _____

▶ Write the contraction that completes each sentence.

13. Will Jack and Jenna help us with the yardwork?

    Of course, _____ do it.

14. Where is the stapler? _____ the stapler.

15. When will we eat? _____ eat now.

16. Is Kyle going to turn his homework in on

    time? _____ better!

▶ Write the following Spelling Words: *what's, aren't, you'd, where's.* Use your best handwriting.

17. _____   19. _____

18. _____   20. _____

SPELLING PRACTICE BOOK   **LESSON 27**

Harcourt

Name _____

▶ Read the paragraph. Write the contraction in place of the words in parentheses.

(There is) a new girl in our class. (She will) be living here for one year. She (does not) know how to speak English. (How is) she going to manage in school? (That is) not a problem. Our class has decided that (we would) like to help her. (Would not) you want someone to do the same for you if you (could not) understand a language in a new place?

1. _____

2. _____

3. _____

4. _____

5. _____

6. _____

7. _____

8. _____

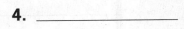
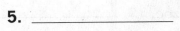

▶ Draw lines through the letters that will be dropped. Then write the contraction for each pair of words below.

9. he is _____

10. they will _____

11. where is _____

12. were not _____

13. you had _____

14. what is _____

15. are not _____

SPELLING WORDS

1. he's
2. couldn't
3. she'll
4. doesn't
5. we'd
6. that's
7. hadn't
8. shouldn't
9. how's
10. weren't
11. there's
12. wouldn't
13. what's
14. where's
15. aren't
16. here's
17. they'll
18. we'll
19. you'd
20. he'd

SPELLING STRATEGY

Placing an Apostrophe

In a contraction, insert an apostrophe in place of any missing letters.

Harcourt

SPELLING WORDS

1. he's
2. couldn't
3. she'll
4. doesn't
5. we'd
6. that's
7. hadn't
8. shouldn't
9. how's
10. weren't
11. there's
12. wouldn't
13. what's
14. where's
15. aren't
16. here's
17. they'll
18. we'll
19. you'd
20. he'd

▶ **Unscramble the Contractions** Rearrange the letters to write a contraction. Add an apostrophe in the correct place.

1. seh _____ **3.** dahtn _____

2. reenwt _____ **4.** eshtre _____

▶ **Make a Replacement** Write a contraction to replace a pair of words in each sentence. Underline the two words.

5. That is my friend in the car. _____

6. Ask if there is a telephone that we can use. _____

7. I had not thought of that! _____

8. He had already arrived. _____

9. We will take a bus to the zoo. _____

10. Here is a ticket for each student. _____

▶ **Similarities** Write the Spelling Word that fits best in each set of words.

11. they'd   you'd   he'd   _____

12. what's   where's   who's   _____

▶ **Rhyme Time** Write the three Spelling Words that rhyme.

13. _____

14. _____

15. _____

Harcourt

Name_____

Related Words

▶ **Write the Spelling Word and its related word for each mini-definition.**

to split into pieces

1. _____   2. _____

to tell about using details

3. _____   4. _____

a match between two teams

5. _____   6. _____

a form that someone fills out

7. _____   8. _____

to broadcast

9. _____   10. _____

pure

11. _____   12. _____

lovely; stunning

13. _____   14. _____

▶ **Write the Spelling Word that fits the word group.**

15. add, subtract, divide   _____

16. crash, slam, hit   _____

▶ **Write the following Spelling Words:** *collision,*
multiplication, bounty, bountiful. **Use your best**
handwriting.

17. _____   19. _____

18. _____   20. _____

Harcourt

SPELLING WORDS

1. describe
2. description
3. nature
4. natural
5. televise
6. television
7. apply
8. application
9. compete
10. competition
11. divide
12. division
13. beauty
14. beautiful
15. collide
16. collision
17. multiply
18. multiplication
19. bounty
20. bountiful

Handwriting
Tip: Be sure
to use one
overcurve
joining stroke
before forming
the letter *n.*
Otherwise, the
n could look like
an *m.*

_____

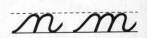

SPELLING WORDS

1. describe
2. description
3. nature
4. natural
5. televise
6. television
7. apply
8. application
9. compete
10. competition
11. divide
12. division
13. beauty
14. beautiful
15. collide
16. collision
17. multiply
18. multiplication
19. bounty
20. bountiful

SPELLING STRATEGY

Related Words

Check your spelling of all words that are related to a root word.

▶ **Read the television sports broadcast. Circle the eight misspelled words. Then write the words correctly.**

Davision Compatition

FIRST PLACE

#1

Athletes will compeat next month in the 33rd regional track meet. If you want to aply, please do so right away. Local sports reporters will be there to discribe the meet. The meet will be sponsored by the Nachural Foods Corporation. Winners will devide up the prize money. Be sure to get your aplication in before November 3rd.

1. _____
2. _____
3. _____
4. _____
5. _____
6. _____
7. _____
8. _____

▶ **For each Spelling Word listed below, write the Spelling Word that contains the same root word or root.**

9. describe _____

10. natural _____

11. television _____

12. division _____
13. beautiful _____
14. bounty _____

Harcourt

▶ **Try It Out** Write the Spelling Words that fit each clue.

These six words end with the long sound of the vowel *i*.

1. _____

2. _____

3. _____

4. _____

5. _____

6. _____

These fours words end with *-tion*.

7. _____

8. _____

9. _____

10. _____

These two words end with the long sound of the vowel *e*.

11. _____

12. _____

These two words end with the suffix *-ful*.

13. _____

14. _____

▶ **Fun with Words** Inside each word shape, write the Spelling Word that fits.

15.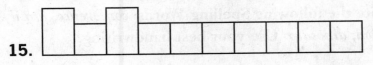

16.

SPELLING WORDS
1. describe
2. description
3. nature
4. natural
5. televise
6. television
7. apply
8. application
9. compete
10. competition
11. divide
12. division
13. beauty
14. beautiful
15. collide
16. collision
17. multiply
18. multiplication
19. bounty
20. bountiful

Harcourt

SPELLING WORDS

1. industry
2. buffalo
3. exciting
4. terrible
5. electric
6. dangerous
7. exercise
8. horizon
9. favorite
10. library
11. substitute
12. typical
13. dinosaur
14. curious
15. average
16. period
17. amazement
18. bicycle
19. conference
20. family

Handwriting Tip: Be sure to make a loop at the top and the bottom when writing the letter *f*. Otherwise, the *f* could look like a *j*.

Words with Three Syllables

▶ **Write a Spelling Word to complete each sentence.**

Shows about cowboys are always **(1)** _____ .

Actors in these shows get plenty of **(2)** _____ .

However, it can be **(3)** _____ work. One

night, a **(4)** _____ got loose. It was

(5) _____ ! To everyone's

(6) _____ , no one was hurt. It was

not a **(7)** _____ Wild West show.

▶ **Write the Spelling Word that goes with each mini-definition.**

8. preferred above all _____

9. a type of transportation _____

10. a place where books can be borrowed _____

11. a replacement _____

12. having power _____

13. where earth and sky meet _____

14. commerce and production _____

15. interested, intrigued _____

16. common, usual _____

▶ **Write the following Spelling Words:** *conference, family, period, dinosaur.* **Use your best handwriting.**

17. _____   19. _____

18. _____   20. _____

SPELLING PRACTICE BOOK   **LESSON 29**

Harcourt

Name _____

► **Read the signs below. Circle the eight misspelled words. Then write each word correctly.**

| Exercize Room | 1. _____ |

| Children's Liberry | 2. _____ |

| Danjerous! Electrik Wires | 3. _____ |
| | 4. _____ |

| Fanny's Faverite Flavors Ice Cream Parlor | 5. _____ |

| Industree Avenue | 6. _____ |

| Bycycle Path | 7. _____ |

| Conferance Room | 8. _____ |

► **Find the word in each pair that looks right. Then circle the one that looks wrong. Write the word that is correct.**

9. bufallo   buffalo   _____

10. typical   tipical   _____

11. ekciting   exciting   _____

12. terrible   terible   _____

13. substitoot   substitute   _____

14. horizen   horizon   _____

15. curious   cureous   _____

1. industry
2. buffalo
3. exciting
4. terrible
5. electric
6. dangerous
7. exercise
8. horizon
9. favorite
10. library
11. substitute
12. typical
13. dinosaur
14. curious
15. average
16. period
17. amazement
18. bicycle
19. conference
20. family

SPELLING STRATEGY

Comparing Spellings

When you're not sure how to spell a word, try spelling it in different ways. Compare the spellings, and choose the one that looks correct.

Harcourt

SPELLING WORDS

1. industry
2. buffalo
3. exciting
4. terrible
5. electric
6. dangerous
7. exercise
8. horizon
9. favorite
10. library
11. substitute
12. typical
13. dinosaur
14. curious
15. average
16. period
17. amazement
18. bicycle
19. conference
20. family

▶ **Use the Clues** Write the Spelling Word that fits each clue.

These two words have double consonants.

1. _____

2. _____

These seven words end with the letter *e*.

3. _____

4. _____

5. _____

6. _____

7. _____

8. _____

9. _____

▶ **Mystery Vowels** For each ?, think of the missing vowel. Then write the Spelling Word.

10. d?n?s??r   _____

11. ?m?z?m?nt   _____

12. f?m?l?   _____

13. s?bst?t?t?   _____

14. p?r??d   _____

15. h?r?z?n   _____

Harcourt

Name _____

Words from Spanish

SPELLING WORDS
1. canyon
2. tornado
3. breeze
4. cafeteria
5. coyote
6. tomato
7. barbecue
8. mosquito
9. plaza
10. pueblo
11. chili
12. alligator
13. rodeo
14. patio
15. bonanza
16. avocado
17. mesa
18. burro
19. enchilada
20. burrito

▶ **Write the Spelling Word that goes with each clue.**

1. an insect  _____

2. a dwelling or village _____

3. a plump, juicy fruit _____

4. a violent windstorm _____

5. a meal cooked over fire _____

6. a deep valley with steep sides _____

7. a public square _____

8. a wolflike animal _____

9. an outdoor sitting area _____

10. a hot, spicy soup _____

11. cheese wrapped in a tortilla
    and baked in sauce _____

12. a cool, pleasant wind _____

13. a fruit with dark
    green skin _____

14. something that provides wealth _____

15. where you eat at school _____

16. a hill with a flat top
    and a steep side _____

▶ **Write the following Spelling Words:** *rodeo, burrito,*
burro, alligator. **Use your best handwriting.**

17. _____   19. _____

18. _____   20. _____

Handwriting Tip: Remember to curve up and then down twice to make the letter *r.* Otherwise, the letters *or* could look like *oi.*

_____

or oi

Harcourt

SPELLING WORDS

1. canyon
2. tornado
3. breeze
4. cafeteria
5. coyote
6. tomato
7. barbecue
8. mosquito
9. plaza
10. pueblo
11. chili
12. alligator
13. rodeo
14. patio
15. bonanza
16. avocado
17. mesa
18. burro
19. enchilada
20. burrito

SPELLING STRATEGY

Comparing Spellings

Spell a word in different ways, compare the spellings, and choose the one that looks right to you.

▶ **Read the postcard. Circle the twelve misspelled words. Then write the words correctly.**

Cary Ciyote
18 Canyun Road
Pweblo, Colorado 81005

Dear Cary,

Having a good time except for getting a mosqito bite every ten seconds! Went to a barbequ in the plasa. Enjoyed the cool breze and the tomayto chily! I got a job in the school cafiteria. Heard there was a turnado near your house. Hope you're okay.

Amos Alligater

1. _____ 7. _____

2. _____ 8. _____

3. _____ 9. _____

4. _____ 10. _____

5. _____ 11. _____

6. _____ 12. _____

▶ **Find the word in each group that looks right. Then circle the ones that look wrong. Write the word that is correct.**

13. bonansa bonaza bonanza _____

14. buro burro burroe _____

15. pateo patio patyo _____

Harcourt

Name_____

▶ **Fun with Words** Write the Spelling Word that names each picture.

1. _____

2. _____

3. _____

4. _____

5. _____

6. _____

▶ **Categories** Write the Spelling Words that fit in each category.

Food Words

7. _____   11. _____

8. _____   12. _____

9. _____   13. _____

10. _____

Geographic Words

14. _____   15. _____

Harcourt

Name _____

Practice Test

► **Read each group of words. Find the word that is spelled correctly. Fill in the letter for that word.**

1. (A) pome
   (B) poam
   (C) poem
   (D) peom

2. (F) shouldn't
   (G) shuoldn't
   (H) shouldnt'
   (J) shoudno't

3. (A) were'nt
   (B) wer'nt
   (C) weren't
   (D) we'rnt

4. (F) vilin
   (G) violine
   (H) vialin
   (J) violin

5. (A) describe
   (B) discribe
   (C) descrebe
   (D) describ

6. (F) compete
   (G) compeat
   (H) compeet
   (J) compet

7. (A) applie
   (B) aply
   (C) apply
   (D) appley

8. (F) electrick
   (G) electric
   (H) elektrik
   (J) electrik

9. (A) chilie
   (B) chillee
   (C) chilley
   (D) chili

10. (F) tomato
    (G) tomatoe
    (H) tomaito
    (J) tamato

11. (A) leotord
    (B) leotard
    (C) leatard
    (D) leatord

12. (F) avacado
    (G) avocado
    (H) avacodoe
    (J) avacadoe

Harcourt

REVIEW

Name _____

▶ **Read each set of phrases. Find the underlined word that is spelled incorrectly. Fill in the oval next to the group of words with the misspelled word.**

1. ⬭ a <u>crewl</u> joke   ⬭ turn the <u>dial</u>
   ⬭ the <u>nucleus</u> of the cell

2. ⬭ it <u>doesn't</u> work   ⬭ a <u>trial</u> run
   ⬭ <u>their's</u> no need for that

3. ⬭ the plane needs <u>fuel</u>   ⬭ <u>hows</u> your mom
   ⬭ <u>wouldn't</u> dream of it

4. ⬭ <u>that's</u> all   ⬭ give a <u>description</u>
   ⬭ <u>hes'</u> right about that

5. ⬭ a <u>competetion</u>   ⬭ <u>televise</u> the show
   ⬭ a balanced <u>diet</u>

6. ⬭ a new <u>television</u> set   ⬭ <u>division</u> facts
   ⬭ the automobile <u>industrie</u>

7. ⬭ at the <u>libary</u>   ⬭ on the <u>horizon</u>
   ⬭ where the <u>buffalo</u> roam

8. ⬭ <u>mosquito</u> bites   ⬭ a <u>substitute</u> teacher
   ⬭ good <u>exersise</u>

9. ⬭ a <u>terrible</u> mistake   ⬭ <u>cafiteria</u> food
   ⬭ a <u>dangerous</u> animal

10. ⬭ an <u>aligator</u>   ⬭ a <u>natural</u> smile
    ⬭ what an <u>exciting</u> movie

11. ⬭ a good <u>influence</u>   ⬭ a <u>violant</u> outburst
    ⬭ the sleepy <u>koala</u>

12. ⬭ <u>youd</u> better be there   ⬭ <u>what's</u> the big deal
    ⬭ <u>we'll</u> see

13. ⬭ a <u>bountiful</u> harvest   ⬭ such <u>beautiful</u> flowers
    ⬭ two cars <u>colide</u>

14. ⬭ most ferocious <u>dinosaur</u>   ⬭ a <u>curious</u> cat
    ⬭ speak at a <u>conferance</u>

Spelling Table

THE SPELLING TABLE below lists all the sounds that we use to speak the words of English. Each first column of the table gives the pronunciation symbol for a sound, such as **ō**. Each second column of the table gives an example of a common word in which this sound appears, such as *open* for the /ō/ sound. Each third column of the table provides examples of the ways that the sound can be spelled, such as *oh, o, oa, ow, ough, oe,* and *o–e* for the /ō/ sound.

The Sound	As In	Can Be Spelled
a	add	cat
ā	age	game, rain, day, paper
ä	palm	ah, father, dark, heart
â(r)	care	dare, fair, where, bear, their
b	bat	big, cabin, rabbit
ch	check	chop, march, catch
d	dog	dig, bad, ladder, called
e	egg	end, met, ready, any, said, says, friend
ē	be	she, see, people, key, field, city
f	fit	five, offer, cough, photo
g	go	gate, bigger
h	hot	hope, who
i	it	inch, hit, pretty, been, busy
ī	ice	item, fine, pie, buy, high, try, dye, eye
j	joy	jump, gem, magic, cage, edge
k	keep	king, cat, lock
l	look	let, ball

SPELLING TABLE

Harcourt

The Sound	As In	Can Be Spelled
m	**m**ove	**m**ake, ha**mm**er
n	**n**ice	**n**ew, ca**n**, fu**nn**y, **kn**ow, **gn**ome
ng	ri**ng**	thi**ng**, to**ngue**
o	**o**dd	p**o**t, h**o**nor
ō	**o**pen	**oh**, **o**ver, g**o**, **oa**k, gr**ow**, th**ough**, t**oe**, b**o**ne
ô	d**o**g	f**o**r, m**o**re, r**oa**r, b**a**ll, w**a**lk, d**aw**n, f**au**lt, br**oa**d, **ough**t
oi	**oi**l	n**oi**se, t**oy**
o͝o	t**oo**k	f**oo**t, w**ou**ld, w**o**lf, p**u**ll
o͞o	p**oo**l	c**oo**l, l**o**se, s**ou**p, thr**ough**, d**ue**, fr**ui**t, dr**ew**
ou	**ou**t	**ou**nce, n**ow**
p	**p**ut	**p**in, ca**p**, ha**pp**y
r	**r**un	**r**ed, ca**r**, hu**rr**y, **wr**ist
s	**s**ee	**s**it, **sc**ene, lo**ss**, li**s**ten, **c**ity
sh	ru**sh**	**sh**oe, **s**ure, o**c**ean, spe**ci**al, mi**ss**ion
t	**t**op	**t**an, kep**t**, be**tt**er, walk**ed**, caugh**t**
th	**th**in	**th**ink, clo**th**
th̶	**th**is	**th**ese, clo**th**ing
u	**u**p	c**u**t, b**u**tter, s**o**me, fl**oo**d, d**oe**s, y**ou**ng
û(r)	b**ur**n	t**ur**n, b**ir**d, w**or**k, **ear**ly, h**er**d
v	**v**ery	**v**ote, o**v**er, o**f**
w	**w**in	**w**ait, t**w**ins
y	**y**et	**y**ear, on**i**on
yo͞o	**u**se	**c**ue, f**ew**
z	**z**oo	**z**ebra, la**z**y, bu**zz**, wa**s**, sci**ss**ors, the**se**
zh	vi**s**ion	gara**g**e, televi**si**on
ə		**a**bout, list**e**n, penc**i**l, mel**o**n, circ**u**s

Harcourt

Spelling Strategies

Let us show you some of our favorite spelling strategies!

Here's a tip that helps me spell a word. I **say** the word. Then I **picture** the way it is spelled. Then I **write** it!

When I'm learning how to spell a word, the **Study Steps to Learn a Word** are a big help. See pages 8 and 9.

I think of ways to spell the vowel sounds in a word. Then I **try different spellings** until the word looks right.

When I don't know how to spell a word, I sometimes just take my best **guess!** Then I **check** it in a **dictionary** or a **thesaurus**.

Sometimes I **proofread** a sentence **backward.** I start with the last word and end with the first word. It really helps me notice words I've misspelled! Then I proofread for meaning.

Harcourt

I **proofread** my work **twice.** First, I circle words I know are misspelled. Then, I look for words I'm not sure of.

When I write a word that is a **homophone,** I make sure the word I've written makes sense.

When I'm writing a **compound word,** I think about how the **two smaller words** are spelled.

Sometimes thinking of a **rhyming word** helps me figure out how to spell a word.

I think about **spelling rules,** such as how to change a word's spelling before adding *-ed* or *-ing*.

Drawing the **shape** of a word helps me remember its spelling. This is the shape of the word *yellow.*

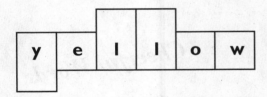

When I **proofread,** I like to **work with a partner.** First, I read the words aloud as my partner looks at the spelling. Then we switch jobs.

Harcourt

My Spelling Log

WHAT'S A SPELLING LOG? It's a special place where you can keep track of words that are important to you. Look at what you'll find in your Spelling Log!

Spelling Words to Study

This is a great place for you to list the Spelling Words you need to study. There is a column for each theme of your spelling book.

My Own Word Collection

Be a word collector, and keep your collection here! Sort words you want to remember into fun categories you make up yourself!

Sound Words

Cheerful Words

Social Studies Words

Vacation Words

Music Words

Funny Words

Animal Words

Math Words

Harcourt

Spelling Words to Study

List the words from each lesson that need your special attention. Be sure to list the words that you misspelled on the Pretest.

Theme 1	Theme 2
Words with Short Vowels	Endings /zhər/ and /chər/
Words with Long *a*, *e*, and *i*	Words Ending in *-ed* and *-ing*
Words with Long *o* and *u*	Unstressed Endings /ən/ and /ər/
Vowels Before *r*	Unstressed Ending /əl/
Words with /s/, /z/, and /sh/	Plurals

Harcourt

Spelling Words to Study

Theme 3	Theme 4
Words with "Silent" Letters	Suffixes -able and -less
Compound Words	Suffixes -eer, -ist, -ian, -or, and -er
Troublesome Words and Phrases	Prefixes non-, in-, and un-
Suffixes -ant and -ent	Prefixes re- and inter-
Suffixes -tion and -ness	Prefixes dis- and de-

Harcourt

Spelling Words to Study

Theme 5	Theme 6
Prefixes *pre-* and *pro-*	VV Words
VCCV Words	Contractions
More Words with *-ed* and *-ing*	Related Words
VCCCV Words	Words with Three Syllables
VCV Words	Words from Spanish

Harcourt

My Own Word Collection

When you read and listen, be on the lookout for words you want to remember. Group them into categories any way you like, and write them on these pages. Pretty soon you'll have a word collection of your very own!

Harcourt

My Own Word Collection

Save words you really like. Include words you have trouble pronouncing or spelling.

My Own Word Collection

Add a clue beside a word to help you remember it. The clue might be a picture, a sentence, a definition, or just a note.

Harcourt

Handwriting
Manuscript Alphabet

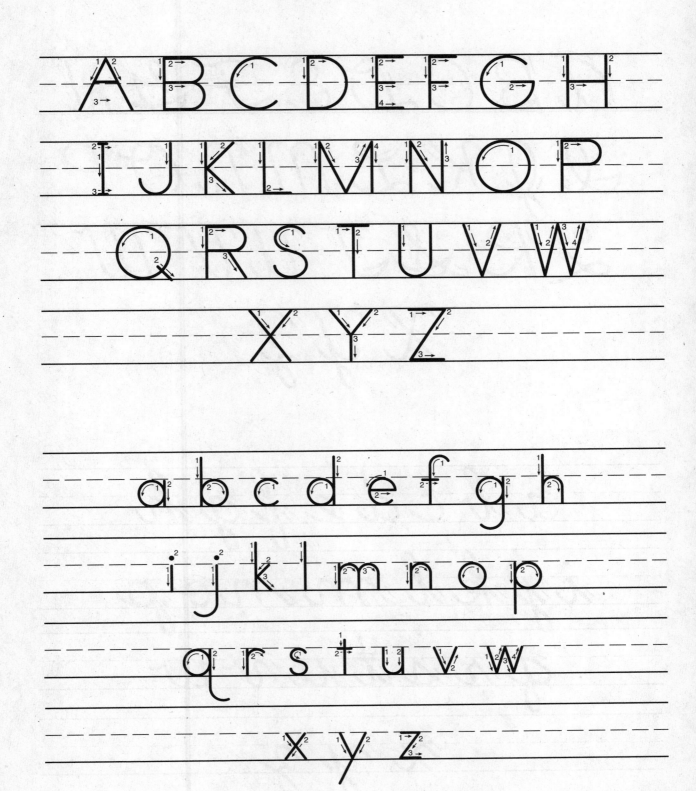

Handwriting
Cursive Alphabet

A B C D E F G H

I J K L M N O P

Q R S T U V W

X Y Z

a b c d e f g h

i j k l m n o p

q r s t u v w

x y z

Harcourt

HANDWRITING MODELS

Handwriting
D'Nealian Manuscript Alphabet

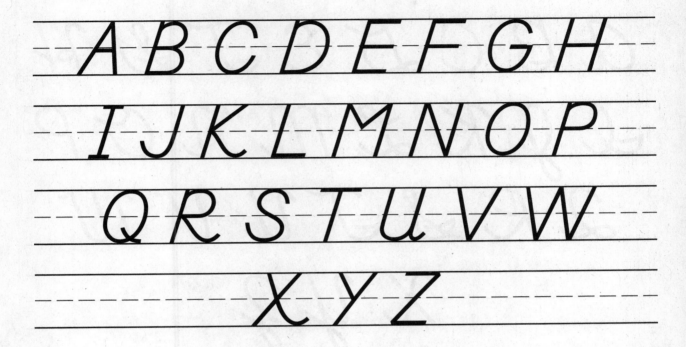

A B C D E F G H
I J K L M N O P
Q R S T U V W
X Y Z

a b c d e f g h
i j k l m n o p
q r s t u v w
x y z

Harcourt

Handwriting
D'Nealian Cursive Alphabet

A B C D E F G H

I J K L M N O P

2 R S T U V W

X Y Z

a b c d e f g h

i j k l m n o p

q r s t u v w

x y z

Harcourt

HANDWRITING MODELS